Make Your Small Business Communications Ecosystem Thrive

First Printing, 2014

Printed in the United States of America

ISBN 978-1499379464

Register This Book and Get Free Updates and Free Videos

To get updates to this book and access to our videos that will show you how to grow your business with the strategies in this book, plus an invitation to interactive online livecasts to meet the author and his team, visit:

- http://os4.com/r/TEAM1, or
- text "telecom" and your email to 58885, or
- text your email address to (510) 574-7500, or
- scan this QR Code:

Make Your Small Business Communications Ecosystem Thrive

How to Gain a Competitive Advantage Using New Telecommunications Technologies

Paul J. Svec

vi

Table of Contents

About the Author

Paul J. Svec, CEO and co-founder of Team One Solutions, Inc. of San Leandro, CA, has 40 years of telecom industry experience spanning the full range of sales, management and executive roles. Paul has managed both direct and distribution business units for large international and national corporations such as NEC America and ROLM Corporation. He honed his entrepreneurial skills with a start-up MPLS network management company, AON Networks, as well as his own successful telecom business, PhoneMaster Communications. Paul is responsible for the day to day executive management of Team One Solutions.

When not running the company, Paul and Dana are enthusiasts in the theater and arts community in San Francisco. Grandchildren, biking, hiking, birding, and our boxer Cassius fill up the weekend agendas. We really love to cook for our family and friends and can usually include some of our own produce from our garden.

You can reach Paul through any of the following media:

Website: **http://TeamOneSolutions.com**
Email: **paul@TeamOneSolutions.com**
Phone: **510-357-5555**

Foreword

Satisfying customers today is tougher than ever, and merely satisfying them is not enough. You want your customers to love you, and to be great references for other prospective customers. In "How to Make Your Small Business Communications Ecosystem Thrive", Paul Svec provides a proven roadmap to use all facets of modern business communications tools to attract customers, to retain them, and to enable you to grow your business with the help of your customers.

I had the privilege of working with Paul as the Vice President and Western Region, U.S. Manager for ROLM Corporation – developer of the first digital PBX. Before that, I spent several years as the General Counsel for the company, and then became the startup General Manager of ROLM's Northern California (Silicon Valley and San Francisco Bay Area) Operating Company. Paul was a senior account manager in our Operating Company, and later enjoyed a very successful career as a Sales Manager.

In my early years working with Paul, I found the technical details of the PBX business to be quite complex, but even then Paul had a straightforward way of simplifying the concepts so that customers readily grasped why our solutions were better than those of our competition. In this book, Paul explains with great clarity and insight the use of modern communications tools – voice and data technologies, computer and network devices and software, and social media – to make fast and informed decisions about your business.

It was a pleasure to work with Paul 30 years ago, and it is terrific to find him today at the vanguard of 21st century communications tools. His comprehensive grasp of the information technologies discussed in this book will help many business owners and managers gain a competitive edge in the marketplace.

Bill Friedman
Founder and CEO of NetFlow Logic Corporation
(www.netflowlogic.com)
Atherton, California

Introduction

What separates the successful businesses from the ordinary? Why do some organizations thrive in good times and bad and others flounder and fail? Everyone who has ever owned, operated, or managed a business has asked themselves those questions many, many times.

If we discount the effects of luck, timing, and unlimited capital resources (which leaves us with the large majority of business owners) the answer is clearly the ability to make a **lot of informed decisions whenever they need to be made.**

This is a simple concept, but one that requires fortitude and information that not every business owner and manager may possess. All business owners, myself included, make scores, hundreds of decisions that affect our businesses; who to hire, how to acquire financing, which vendors to partner with, how to acquire and retain our clients, what type of marketing plans to use, where to locate, etc. Chances are good, but not guaranteed, that the more informed you were when you made a decision, the better the outcome.

As important, and maybe more so, is our willingness and ability to make these decision(s) quickly. Faster than our competitors, before we miss a fleeting opportunity, ahead of the market. Not reckless, but agile and informed decisions win the day and the war.

I wrote this book to give business owners, managers, investors, and key employees the tools to help them make the best possible and timely decisions about the glue that enables all business to operate, your communications ecosystem. Your ecosystem encompasses every category of communication: voice, data, video, social media, and all of their components; phones, computers, smartphones, email, IM, application and storage servers, LAN/WAN, bandwidth. And the myriad business applications that run on them. And the people that design, operate, and maintain them.

These systems tie your clients, employees, partners, and vendors to your organization. And your organization will thrive, or not, in direct relationship to your understanding and optimization of these resources.

If we've done a good job with this book you will be able to develop a communications strategy to take advantage of the tremendous advances in technology that our industry has to offer. And you will gain the confidence to make informed decisions ahead of the pack, decisions that will give your business a distinct competitive advantage.

Paul Svec
San Leandro, CA
June 2014

1 | Why Develop a Telecom Strategy?

The question "Is creating a telecommunications strategy important for my business?" could sound rhetorical, but it's not. The one system that ties you, your managers, your staff, your vendors and your clients together is your communications system. However, in many small- and medium-sized businesses (SMBs), the subject of communications is often taken for granted. You may have purchased your telephone system ten years ago and it's working. You don't think you need to think about that any longer. You probably installed a Local Area Network (LAN) when you moved into your building five years ago, and you attached PCs, servers, and storage devices to it, and you have a network administrator who keeps the network running along for you. That's typically been the view that many small- or medium-sized business owners have had about their communication systems, but today, those systems have become a lot more involved than the simple local area network and the phone system.

So why would you want to take another harder and more in-depth look about what you have and what you don't have? We discovered over the years that businesses that win and grow do it in large part because their communications systems enable them to communicate better and less expensively, not just internally, but with their clients, their prospective clients, and their vendors, so there's a good business reason to make sure that you understand what systems you have and how they may be helping or hindering your bottom line.

Competitive Differentiation

Perhaps the most compelling reason for creating a telecom strategy is to get a competitive advantage. So how do you do that? Typically, you're going to improve overall productivity, including customer-client relations, vendor relations, and internal communications and collaboration, but how? Here are some answers:

- Your staff is going to be more responsive, both internally and externally with clients and vendors. Products are going to get to market faster, and sales are going to close faster.
- You're going to connect questions with experts that can answer them in a timely fashion.
- You're going to enable your clients, vendors, and staff to communicate with you via voice, voicemail, text, web, video, IM, chat, and social media, increasing customer satisfaction.

A well-executed telecom strategy can make you more proactive than you might have been in the past. Modern communication systems can enable you to accelerate communications, and allow you to do it better than your competitors.

Your communications systems are no longer commodities and now they're more than just the phone system in the closet and the computer on your desk. They're the network that ties them together, and these systems enable quality communications, internally and externally, with your staff, your clients, your prospects, and your vendors. A well-crafted telecommunications strategy can, and should, be used to give your organization a strategic advantage.

Security Risks

In addition to the business issues or business rationale for fine tuning or improving your systems, security risks have become a bigger part of what we worry about every day in our businesses, and it doesn't matter what kind of business you have - you could be manufacturing a product, or providing professional services, you could be a financial institution, or you could be a healthcare institution - everyone is a target for increased security breaches in their business. Whether that's people hacking into your telephone system to make free long distance calls that you pay for, or whether it's people hacking into your servers to capture your customer client information, the security risks are real and they need to be addressed.

As an example, we have a client that had installed a new telephone system, and they do a ton of business offshore, most of it in China. They recently discovered, actually from us, that many long distance calls were being made from their system but not to their clients. Someone was able to hack into their system and make literally thousands of dollars of international long distance calls.

Why did it happen? Some of the security measures that we had recommended to put into place with the company were not implemented (they are now). We intervened along with the carrier, and we patched up the holes. We've gotten the company to make sure that every employee in the organization now follows the security procedures that they need to. The fraud stopped, the hacking was thwarted and the problem got fixed, at least temporarily. But these sorts of security breaches are not uncommon, and that is something that ownership and management of every company needs to be aware of. Constant vigilance is required.

Regulatory Environment

Increasingly, healthcare and also the financial industry are required by law to do some things with respect to their communications systems that they have not had to do in the past.

For financial institutions, many, if not all, client calls have to be recorded. These calls have to be archived, they have to be stored and they have to be retrievable. Not every communication system is geared up to do this, but it certainly needs to be, even if it's not yet a regulatory requirement.

For healthcare related companies, a wide variety of privacy and security issues come into play in any sort of communications with the patients and the facility. If you operate in this arena, the communication systems that you have will likely need to be modified to comply with the increasingly difficult regulatory requirements.

That's tough stuff. Security risks are scary, as is spending money to comply with regulations from the government.

Assign Responsibility

Another reason for developing a telecommunications strategy is to get very clear about who is leading the effort to accelerate communications, comply with regulations, and protect the organization's proprietary information. Who in your company is responsible for the communications systems that you have in your business? That depends on your organization, and there is no one right answer. Executives, your management team, your CIO if you have one, your IT guy, and the finance department, of course, all play a role. Increasingly, sales and marketing will have, and should have, more input into what your systems look like and how they operate.

Typically, you're also going to have outside suppliers who have a stake in your systems as well, whether that's the vendor that supports your phone system, or whether it's the expert on VMware who is helping you design your servers, or whether it's the carrier who is making sure they are delivering the promised bandwidth to you.

What we have found in our practice is that in the typical SMB, there is a fractured set of stakeholders responsible for the communications systems. Frequently, no one is leading the team to make sure that everything is optimized from the standpoint of what it can do, nor is the system optimized from the standpoint of cost management, with the result that your company may be needlessly harming the bottom line. By helping you craft a telecommunications strategy, this book will give you the tools to help you get control of that process.

Accelerating Change

The pace of technological change in the telecom system marketplace is accelerating. As an example, the traditional sources for getting your telephone system have changed dramatically in the last 30 years. It used to be you got your phone system from the Bell Systems or your local carrier. Then, prominent manufacturers such as Northern Telecom and ROLM came into the market in the 1980's and sold phone systems directly. But now, the manufacturers are relying on value-added resellers, such as Team One Solutions, to sell voice systems to the SMBs, and that voice system may or may not even be on premise any longer.

The local area network system, the firewall, the router and the server that you installed five years ago when you moved into your building also have changed in throughput capacity, security levels, and even whether or not you need to have them in your server room. It used to be that everybody had a Microsoft email exchange server in their building. A lot of that capability now has moved out of your building and into the cloud, and we'll talk about that in more detail later in the book.

Voice and data bandwidth carriers, providers of your connections to the public telephone network and the internet, used to be the domain of only a handful of companies. Now, there are tons of choices for bandwidth, and your requirement for bandwidth has probably increased dramatically in just the past few years. It has increased because of wider usage of your website, smartphones, iPads, wireless access with tablets, and use of video, all requiring more bandwidth in the applications that they access outside of your company. A recent phenomenon in just the past five to seven years is that many organizations have experienced an increased requirement for bandwidth, whether or not their company has grown.

To give you an example, we are working with a company with a dozen or so locations up and down the state of California, and during the last recession, they shrank in size. They went from 300 employees to about a 175. Interestingly, when they started to look at their requirements for both voice and data bandwidth, they found that, in fact, they needed more bandwidth, even though their business had shrunk. This came as a shock to the company's VP Finance, and it occurred for some of the reasons we mentioned before: applications being accessed in the cloud, employees utilizing not just the fixed workstation at their desk, but also their smartphones, their iPads, and tablet computing throughout the organization.

So getting a handle on what your bandwidth needs are and understanding how that impacts your business is a very important consideration.

Faster Communications

Rapid communications, the requirement to react more quickly than you did just a few years ago, is a reality in every single type of business that we know of. Your customers, your clients, and your employees expect your communications to be transparent and almost real time. We don't want to go through an operator to reach a particular staff member: we want their direct number. We don't want to wait four or five hours to get an answer to a question. Your prospects do not want your sales team to spend days or weeks preparing a quotation for what you sell. Your customer service department needs to provide solutions to the problems, questions, and complaints when they come in to your company a lot quicker than they did just a couple of years ago.

What's going to enable that to happen in large part is going to be your communication systems, and if you're going to continue to compete, win and grow in your marketplace, you're going to need to understand that and you're going to need to provide the sort of speed that your clients and your employees are demanding.

Multi-mode Communications

In the not so distant past, business communications used to be conducted by a personal letter, a phone call, and face-to-face meetings. Today, we still have snail-mail and voice, and now we have email, we have video, we have websites, we have chat, instant messaging, texting, and a wide variety of social media, from Facebook to Twitter to LinkedIn and many other social media platforms.

Most companies are going to need almost every one of these modes offered to their vendors, their clients, and their employees. You can't just get away with one or the other. You're going to need to understand and provide many, if not all, of these categories.

Every one of them is going to require some sort of improvement, modification, or addition to your existing communication systems, whether that's beefing up your local area network speed, whether it's adding software or applications to your smartphones and tablet devices, or whether it's adding somebody to your marketing department who understands social media who can help you blend that into your image as a company in your communications with your customers.

You're probably wondering how do you do that without going broke. The cost of a modern communication system and all of the things that go along with it obviously need to be carefully considered. This book will help you to understand the types of communications that will be important for your business and to help you understand how to get best value from the providers of those communication systems and applications and devices.

Keeping Current

You need to acquire some expertise about the types of communications that your company is going to need. Where do you currently get it? Sources of information include internet searches, company staff, and colleagues that may have made some recent improvements or changes in their communication systems. Obviously, another valuable source can be from current vendors that are providing services to you, and often from industry-wide conferences or conventions where these issues are addressed.

This book will provide you with an outline and a methodology for acquiring the information you need to inventory and improve your communication systems in your organization.

Hopefully by now we've made a compelling argument for why you need to have a telecom strategy and not just a disjointed collection of voice and data systems, but a strategy to use those systems together to your advantage. Our goal at Team One Solutions is to assist you in developing that strategy, and developing the strategy that's appropriate for your business objectives.

To get updates to this book and access to our videos that will show you how to grow your business with the strategies in this book, plus an invitation to interactive online livecasts to meet the author and his team, visit:

- http://os4.com/r/TEAM1, or
- text "telecom" and your email to 58885, or
- text your email address to (510) 574-7500, or
- scan this QR Code:

2 | The Telecommunications Ecosystem

THE TELECOMMUNICATIONS ECOSYSTEM

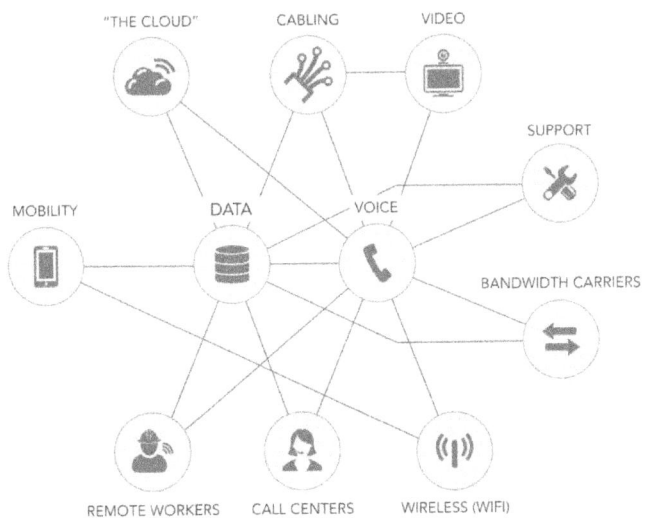

First, we're going to talk about and discuss the many individual components of your telecommunications ecosystem, and if you are like most small organizations, you are going to find out that you have a larger ecosystem than you ever realized.

Communications technology has changed rapidly during the past 10 years, and some of it you'll recognize, but we're going to try to make the point that it all is part of a single ecosystem and you need to understand how it works, how it interacts, and most importantly, how it enables or hinders your business operations, your business growth and your competitiveness.

Voice Systems

Overview

Let's start with your voice systems. This is an area that most SMBs are somewhat familiar with. Voice services can be both synchronous and asynchronous. These are fancy terms, but you'll recognize the functionality. Your voice system is typically going to be a PBX (Private Branch Exchange) that you have located somewhere in your server room, or it can be offsite, and it's a synchronous system in that it allows real-time communications between people within and outside your organization.

In addition to that, you may have a voicemail system which allows for asynchronous or non-real time communications. The voicemail system also includes your auto-attendant functionality, which is an automated way you can choose to greet incoming callers, either all the time or after hours, depending on how you've decided to run your voice communications in your particular business.

Another voice system which has become a necessity recently is voice recording, whereby conversations can be recorded, archived, and retrieved as needed. Voice recording is predominantly used in financial and health care organizations, where this functionality is mandated, but many other organizations are implementing it as well.

Voice systems have changed wildly over the last ten years or so, and we will get into more detail later, but they used to be analog, then they became digital in the 1980s through the 1990s with the advent of TDM (Time Division Multiplexing). Now, newer systems are mostly voice over IP (VoIP), and some of these VoIP systems have even escaped the server room on your premises and now are often found somewhere in the cloud, which we discuss in the next several sections. This latter technology is called "hosted" voice. But the basic functionality is the same: real-time voice communications between two or more people, and asynchronous messages that can be retrieved later.

VoIP

In voice systems today, the leading technology is voice over IP (VoIP), which simply means carrying voice conversations internally and externally over Internet Protocol. It's a technology that began in earnest in the business marketplace about 12 to 15 years ago. The majority of all new voice systems installed in businesses of any size today are VoIP. It doesn't yet have 100% of the market share, but it's getting there.

The reason that it's made an impact, outside of an enormous marketing push by manufacturers and carriers alike, is that there are significant economies in having your voice communications carried over the same local area network and wide area network as your data systems and your data streams.

As an example, a single cable to the desk can now carry both voice and all of your office computing requirements as well: voice and data over the same wiring infrastructure. This simplifies manageability and if you design it, buy it, and install it correctly, it will be a time saver for your IT staff. Your voice and data infrastructure will be in a single view rather than a totally separate system for voice and a totally separate system for data.

Are there any downsides to having a VoIP system, and is it right for everybody? Let's start with the number one downside with VoIP by using the example of Skype and Vonage. Those are two early providers of VoIP services primarily for the residential market, but in some respects for business as well. Skype has made a big push to get into the business marketplace. If you've ever used either one of those services or talked to anybody that does, you may not have always had a great experience. The voice might be choppy. There might be echo on the line. There might be some jitter in the conversation and in some cases if the internet connection is not strong enough and broad enough, that call might drop. For residential applications that's probably not a big issue, especially if it costs less than half of what a normal analog voice line might cost from AT&T. But for businesses, that can be a big concern. Businesses that depend heavily on the quality of the voice communications with their clients and vendors need to understand that not every VoIP system is the same, and not every design of a VoIP system will provide the same quality of experience that you probably want to have.

The point is that designing and implementing a VoIP system that provides a consistently high quality experience requires expertise in the integration of several different technologies. It requires choosing the right technology mix, the right manufacturers, the right carriers, and the right integrators.

When VoIP Isn't Necessary

There might be some circumstances where a VoIP system is either not necessary or may cost more than you need to spend. To give you a couple of examples, if you've been in your building for ten years or longer and you've got an old telephone system that is starting to break down, you can't get repair service, and parts are difficult to find, you're probably looking at replacing it. Your choices are going to be digital or VoIP technology to replace it.

If you have a single location and you don't have any network reasons to put in a VoIP system, you might want to just consider a hybrid. There are several major manufacturers that offer hybrid systems that you could take a look at.

What do we mean by a hybrid system? A hybrid system offers both digital and VoIP technology. You use digital where it makes the most sense and if you've got some remote users or office workers who work out of their home or travel a lot, you might want to take advantage of some of the VoIP functionality in that same system.

The savings on reusing existing cabling, and sometimes even the same phones, can make the difference between the economic viability of replacing your phone system or not. You need to take a look at that, and your value added reseller can help to point you in the right direction. Hybrid systems for many small businesses are occasionally the best choice if you only have one location.

Messaging and Call Recording

The messaging choices that we have today are multiple, and they include your good old standby voicemail we're all familiar with. Voicemail is no longer an isolated storage place for a message someone left you in non-real time. Voicemail now can be viewed, accessed and dealt with in a unified communications (UC) platform, which we discuss in more detail below.

An example is the ability to see your voicemail indicator in your Exchange Outlook account. You may get an email message that will tell you that you have a voicemail or fax, and then you can listen to it, may even read a transcribed version of it, view it, delete it, transfer it, store it, or put it in a file, the same way you would any email message.

Call recording is becoming increasingly important for any regulated business, finance, and healthcare in particular. It's not a want, it's a must, and call recording includes not just the capability to record a voice conversation, but how you store it, how long do you store it, where you store it, how you archive it, how you retrieve the call recordings that are important to you.

Multiple Locations

Organizations with multiple locations will generally discover that the implementation of VoIP often creates a compelling case to adopt a VoIP system. There is really no better way to connect three to a hundred offices in an enterprise together than using VoIP technology. You can securely and easily connect multiple locations to act as a single system using VoIP technology. Frankly, this is where we recommend VoIP systems for our clients. It's enough of an important driver to make that decision as opposed to any of the older digital technologies for networking locations together.

Hosted or On-Premise

We'll talk about computing in the cloud a bit later, but for voice, this is an area where, in general and with some important exceptions, we don't believe the technology has caught up with the requirements for quality or financial performance for the average small- and medium-sized business user in the cloud.

Let's take a look at two systems, one is customer premise-based equipment (CPE), in other words, in your building, and the other one is the exact same system with the same feature set, in fact, even the same phones, and we'll make this as apples for apples as we can, located in the cloud.

The companies that would like you to use the cloud, or hosted, version will tell you that you don't want to have the responsibility or the capital expenditure of having that system in your server room. Why not instead rent it from them and connect to it through either a managed or an unmanaged internet pipe (we'll talk about the differences of those two in a bit).

The premise people will tell you, "You don't want to do that because if you buy your system one time, put it in your server room, you own it. It depreciates. You don't have to continue paying for it forever as you would with the same system hosted in the cloud."

The business model for cloud-hosted VoIP is simply this, "We're going to do all of the heavy lifting, provide all the

PBX features, the transfer, the conferencing, the connectivity for long distance to the outside world, we're going to do all of that for you in our huge data center over something called the softswitch. We're going to upgrade it. We're going to do the software patches. We're going to maintain the system. You don't ever have to worry about it, but you may have to pay us $30 per phone per month for as long as you choose to continue using the services."

Under this model, coming up with an ROI on a hosted VoIP system we have found is extremely difficult. Are there exceptions? Yes. If you're a company that's going to go from ten employees to a hundred in the next six months, we're going to recommend that you use a hosted VoIP system. You don't have to buy the hardware that scales to a hundred when you can rent it one seat at a time from a cloud provider. In that circumstance, a hosted VoIP might make a lot of sense.

If you're firing up remote offices, let's say you're a real estate brokerage and you're going to be adding a new real estate office every month for the next three years, a hosted VoIP system might make sense for you. You might be able to get that connectivity and get those remote offices fired up in a hurry, but that might cost you a bit more and it might take you a little bit longer to do than with CPE or customer premise equipment.

So there are circumstances where hosted VoIP will make more sense than others, but, by and large, the average small- and medium-sized business still should be strongly considering on-premise or CPE.

Data Systems

In addition to your voice systems, you've got data systems, which consist of hardware resources that enable software applications to run. These systems can run on both Local Area Networks (LANs) and Wide Area Networks (WANs). The local area network (LAN) is the part of your network that is within the walls of your organization, and the wide area network (WAN) is where you connect to the outside world, transmitting data in both directions in and out of your company.

Common software applications include your operating systems, email management platform, customer relationship management (CRM), accounting systems, enterprise resource planning (ERP), R&D and production, and point-of-sales systems, and many others. These applications can be running onsite, offsite in company rented locations in a data center somewhere, or hosted by third parties, often referred to as "the cloud".

The hardware components of your data systems consist of your computers, servers, printers, wireless access points (APs), firewalls, routers, and switches, and these are all connected locally by your structured cabling system, which we will talk about in the next section.

Your **computers** these days are a moving target. The traditional view is that this is typically a desktop computer, either Windows based or a Mac, that sits on (or under) an employee's desk. That is changing. Employees today frequently have laptops that may or may not be hard-wired when the employee comes to the office, and now, the employee can often get access to needed applications via a tablet or even a smartphone.

Servers are typically centrally located computers that should have both physical and software security, and need to be accessible by authorized users, and secure, both physically and virtually, from unauthorized users. Servers now include your phone system, if you elect to have CPE gear.

The **printer** landscape has also been shifting, with more sophisticated and relatively inexpensive multi-function machines available to users on a network. Capabilities now include faxing, scanning, copying, and even wireless printing as well as standard printing, so it is no longer necessary that every computer have a directly attached printer.

The next item, **data switches**, are very important to properly constructing and sizing your data network. There's the $150 8-port switch that you can buy at Best Buy that will allow you to connect multiple data devices, but you can't manage it, you can't change it very much, and you're not going to get the kind of throughput that you might need in a modern small- and medium-sized business data network.

Business class data switches, for the purpose of a local area network, basically come in two varieties, PoE and non-PoE. (PoE stands for Power over Ethernet), and it's the kind of data switch that provides a certain fixed amount of power to the devices that are connected to it.

A simple example is a VoIP phone. Depending on the manufacturer, type of display, and the standard used by that VoIP phone, it will require a certain amount of power. You need to know how much power, you need to know how that power will be supplied, and how many ports on the data switch will be providing the type of power you need. It can be a little complicated to determine, so you're going to need an expert to help you make that selection.

Another data switch consideration is that the voice and the video connections that go through your data network real time need to have their particular data packets segmented and prioritized over normal data packets. If you don't do that and you don't have a data switch that allows you to do that, you're not going to have high quality voice communications on your data network and you certainly are not going to have an acceptable amount of bandwidth for your video transmissions as well. All modern data switches have the capability that's called QoS (Quality of Service), and simply what that does is it recognizes a particular data stream as either voice or video versus non-voice or video and prioritizes those real-time data streams over normal data transmissions.

As an example, if you have a voice conversation going on at the same time somebody is trying to print something on your network printer, the data switch will, if you have the right data switch and you've configured it correctly, recognize that the data stream for voice will take priority over that request to print a document on your network printer.

It's a very simple example, but you need to make sure that you're using the correct type of data switch. It typically gets a lot more complicated than that. This is just the basic overview for you, but selecting the right type of data switch is key to the success of your overall data networking plan.

A **firewall** is required for voice and data traffic that goes offsite. Interaction with our clients, vendors, customers, and prospects is necessary, of course, but the downside of that connectivity is that security is now a greater concern. We didn't have to worry about it so much 10 or 15 years ago. Today, we are faced with relentless intrusions into not just our personal data, but our business data as well. Your firewall is a very important element in your voice and data ecosystem for security and control. Every business, no matter what you do, what you make, or what you serve, is subject to security breaches. It can be something as simple as someone hacking into your phone system and making unauthorized long distance calls. It can be as sophisticated as a denial of service attack on your business, your website, your email system and these attacks can basically put you out of business for a while or can at least interrupt your business flow. It can be something as serious as a breach in your intellectual property, your client database that the business owners must be concerned about. Therefore, a modern, up-to-date firewall is as important an element in your ecosystem as anything else we'll talk about. The firewalls have to do much more than simply saying, "We're not going to allow this kind of traffic in." They have to be intelligent enough to know what that traffic is, what it contains and it has to enable you as the business owner to manage those data streams in an intelligent way.

Another important piece of equipment in the data system is the **router**. The router tells the WAN which packets of data are voice and which packets are pure data. The reason this is important is that voice, being synchronous, needs to be prioritized in order to provide high quality, or what we refer to as QoS: Quality of Service. If that prioritization isn't enabled, voice traffic can get garbled, with echo, delay, and jitter. We've all dealt with those challenges from time to time, and it's not pretty.

Structured Cabling

To enable your data system and your voice system components to function, you must have a cabling infrastructure, oftentimes referred to as structured cabling. That cabling infrastructure may be either up to date or not, and a lot of organizations take their cabling for granted and don't think about it very much. Part of your cable infrastructure may have been in the building when you leased it, or if you did install your own cabling, you probably had it installed when you moved in and haven't thought about it much since.

We see a lot of cabling challenges when we first meet with a prospective client. The type of cable may be inadequate, it may be installed poorly and even illegally, and it may be mislabeled or unlabeled in the equipment room. You can have excellent phones and computers at the desktop, but if your cable infrastructure is poor, your system won't be reliable.

It is important to understand that modern, high-speed local area networks require a particular category of cable that will allow higher throughput to enable some of the kinds of streaming services, such as high speed internet access, file transfer, and as importantly, quality VoIP communications. If and when you choose to upgrade your communications systems, understand that these components, including phones, computers, wireless access points, printers, and cameras, will likely require cable infrastructure upgrades as well. Cat5e is the minimum standard today, but Cat 6 and 7, as well as fiber optic cable, are also possibilities. Category

6 and 7 are for even higher rates of speed and some shielding to protect them from interference from other radio waves that might be interfering with your data transmission.

Structured cabling includes not just the cable, but the terminating gear that they connect to, including the wall jacks in the space where people will be working, to patch panels in the equipment area, and then the patch cords that connect from the patch panels into the switches, which can be both voice and data switches. It is important that the cables and their connections be installed correctly and carefully, then tested and labelled.

Bandwidth Carriers

When we say "carrier," we can refer to a voice carrier, often referred to as a "telco", a cellphone carrier, which may be the same company (think ATT), or a data carrier, also known as internet service provider (ISP). In the past, they typically were different companies, but now many carriers are combining services. In today's rapidly changing carrier environment, it's important to understand what's new, what's different, what's economical, what technologies can provide higher bandwidth, and who is providing better customer service. It used to be a pretty simple choice between AT&T and one or two Competitive Local Exchange Carriers (CLECs). For example, maybe it was between AT&T versus TelePacific here in the San Francisco Bay Area. But today, with the introduction of newer technologies such as VoIP and SIP trunking, which is a version of IP voice and data trunking, we have a whole new panoply of carriers: companies like Comcast, CBeyond, MegaPath, nexVortex, EtherSpeak, and many more, and in addition to that, all of the traditional carriers, such as Verizon, XO Communications, and AT&T, are offering new types of circuits to you. You need to understand what they are, how they might fit in your business, how they might lower your costs for internet bandwidth and for voice, and maybe more importantly, how they may be enabling you to connect better with your employees, with your clients, and with your vendors. Let's first examine voice carriers.

Voice Carriers

Voice carriers provide connections to their Central Offices (CO) via a number of different kinds of circuits. We'll start with analog trunks. Analog trunks, sometimes known as "business lines", or "measured business lines", and also known as POTS lines (Plain Old Telephone Service) are used for voice and also for alarm circuits and fax machines. The telco may also supply digital trunks, including PRI (Primary Rate Interface), T1, or even DS3. The advantage of these latter types of trunks is that they can carry both voice and data, although the data speeds are now considered rather slow.

Another integrated circuit is called MPLS, which is MultiProtocol Label Switching. It's a circuit that connects multiple locations in your business. It's typically not something you would use if you only have one location, but if you've got two or three locations or more, MPLS provides a controlled and managed circuit to carry voice, data, and if you choose to, video, basically over the same stream and providing the right level of service for each of those different data streams. If you don't have any MPLS circuits, and you have multiple locations, you may want to consider it in the future.

The latest technology offered by carriers for voice traffic is SIP (Session Initiated Protocol) trunking, which interfaces with the latest VoIP telephone switches, and transmits voice via Internet Protocol. This is now the least expensive trunking alternative, but because the technology is so new, there can be a lot of technical challenges which affect call quality. At the time of this writing, it is still very important to make sure that equipment at the customer's premise is engineering-certified to work with the SIP trunks provided by the carrier. Your valued-added reseller, such as Team One Solutions, can provide invaluable insight into which systems are compatible.

Internet Service Carriers

Next we move to internet service. Sorry, but this is going to get a little technical. Our goal though is to arm you with enough knowledge that you can be more familiar with the pros and cons of the types of internet service available to you. Here are the big concepts relating to internet service, and that oftentimes confuse people.

Bandwidth vs Speed

Bandwidth refers to the **capacity** at which data is transmitted or received, and is expressed in bits, or multiples of bits, per time period, typically in seconds. Thus, you can have bandwidth expressed in bits per second (bps), one-thousand bits per second (kbps) or one-million bits per second (Mbps), and so on. See the bandwidth "speedometer" on the next page.

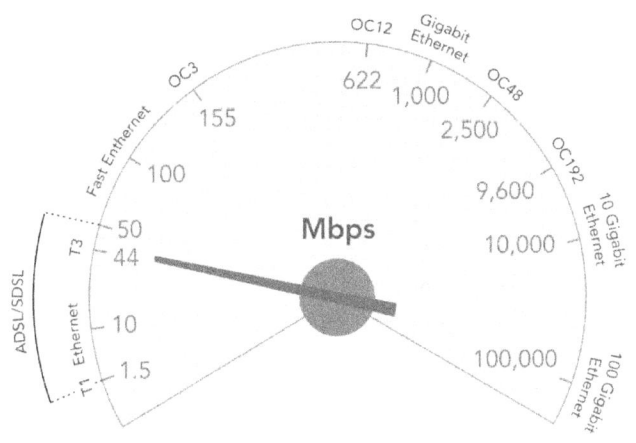

1.5 to 50 Mbps*	ADSL/SDSL*
1.544 Mbit/s	T1/DS1
10 Mbit/s	Ethernet
44.736 Mbit/s	T3/DS3
100 Mbit/s	Fast Ethernet
155 Mbit/s	OC3
622 Mbit/s	OC12
1 Gbit/s	Gigabit Ethernet
2.5 Gbit/s	OC48
9.6 Gbit/s	OC192
10 Gbit/s	10 Gigabit Ethernet
100 Gbit/s	100 Gigabit Ethernet
*Not guaranteed, "best effort only"	*asynchronous/synchronous

It is very important to know that many elements in a data transaction affect the "speed", (sometimes called the **task response time**, "page load" or "user wait" time). Bandwidth, while important, may not be the most important determinant of speed. App turns, RT's (round trips) from application server to user are mathematically more important to the ultimate "speed" of the user experience. The speed of the user device (pc, tablet, smartphone, server) and the speed of the wired and/or wireless LAN are also very important elements in achieving the best possible user response time.

Asynchronous vs Synchronous

Transceiver equipment provided by the carriers can enable either asynchronous or synchronous data transfer. Asynchronous means that there will be a difference between the upload and download speeds, and synchronous means the upload and download speeds are the same.

Medium

This is how your signal, or bandwidth, gets delivered. The primary choices are copper wiring, coaxial cable (also known as coax or simply cable), Ethernet over Copper (EoC) which is a relatively new entrant, fixed wireless, and fiber. Each medium has its own characteristics which affect the bandwidth that can get delivered over that medium, and the bandwidth capability is also determined by the signaling equipment or transceivers at each end of the medium.

Copper is generally regarded as the slowest of the physical mediums, but it is ubiquitous, it is inexpensive, and it's reliable. Recent advancements in transceiver technology have enabled copper networks to operate at Ethernet speeds (10Mbps and higher), but both copper and EoC speeds are limited by distance from the CO.

Coax service, also known as **cable**, is provided by the cable companies, and is almost always asynchronous, since the cable companies are historically downloading video programming, which requires enormous bandwidth to the home or business. The challenge with cable internet service is that it, too, is highly dependent on the distance from the CO, and because it is on a loop with other users, it is also subject to the bandwidth being shared by others on the loop. Therefore, many of the cable companies either won't make a bandwidth speed commitment, or they will provide estimates along with a "best efforts" commitment. Typically, coax can support download speeds from 3Mbps to 10Mbps, and upload speeds from 48kbps to 2.5Mbps.

Fixed wireless is a method whereby ground stations, similar to cell towers, send and receive radio signals with a fixed location. This technology requires line-of-sight between your location and the ground station, and is relatively expensive, but it can be very valuable as a backup, or in areas where it is too expensive to run physical cable. Right now, the upper end on fixed wireless bandwidth is about 10Mbps. The other downside of this technology is that the antennas must be aligned, and the signal can be affected by the weather, including wind and especially rain.

Finally, the gold standard in medium transmission is optical **fiber**. These are thin glass strands that can transmit the highest level of data known on the planet today. Many carriers are investing heavily in installing fiber optic cable in their service areas, especially in heavily populated areas.

When fiber optic service is provided to a location, that location is said to be "lit".

Availability

The availability and choice of internet service depends on a number of factors. The primary consideration is your physical address. You may be in a building or an area where the carriers have not yet delivered their latest services. For example, San Leandro, where our home office is, does not yet have fiber optic service anywhere, even though a number of carriers, especially Comcast, are racing to build out fiber optic networks throughout the Bay Area. In response, a local entrepreneur is building a fixed wireless system and getting local business subscribers. If a carrier has services that are close to your address, but not yet installed, they may offer to provide that service if you, the client, pays the upfront cost of running the service to your building. In many cases, this can add up to thousands of dollars.

Scalability

It is important to understand what your needs are anticipated to be in relation to the service you are contemplating. If you are a six person office whose most common internet task is sending email, getting an inexpensive low-bandwidth service may be just fine. However, if you're a 6 person gaming development start-up anticipating rapid growth, you don't want to even consider a location that doesn't have the option of very high bandwidth, preferably over fiber optic.

Terms

Just as in any vendor relationship, it is very important to consider the terms before contracting with an internet service provider. The prime considerations are how long the contract lasts, typically 1, 2, or 3 years, what the penalties are for terminating the contract, what the guarantees are for the services provided and remedies if expectations are not met, what the pricing is, and what credits might be available for firewalls, routers, and other enabling equipment.

Cell Phone Carriers

Many carriers are offering cell phone plans that can make a big difference to your bottom line. If your level of spending on cellphones has been hidden by being buried in departmental budgets, now may be the time to consider restructuring your cellphone policies. You will want to consider the cell phone signal strength in the service areas in which you operate, especially your physical locations, but you will also want to consider what types of cellphones you want to provide to your staff, the types of plans available, and your flexibility to adjust those plans.

Another important consideration is the ownership of the phones, the phone numbers, and the branding communicated when those phones are used. Many advanced phone systems enable apps on smartphones that enable the employee to call from their cellphone, but display their organization's phone number on Caller ID. If your salespeople are primarily making calls to your prospects and your customers with their personal phones, your customer information may be at risk if that person leaves the organization or the device gets stolen. Many carriers now offer capability to remotely wipe the phones if the device is compromised in any way.

Bundled Services

Many of the carriers available here in the Bay Area are now offering bundles that provide all three services: voice, internet, and cell service. Consolidating the number of vendors you deal with has some significant advantages that may not only be less expensive but may also provide a higher level of overall service.

Yes, carrier selection is a complicated area that a value-added reseller like Team One Solutions will be able to help you work your way through and make sure that your carrier selection, and your carrier product selection, makes the most sense for your business.

Mobility

Some people in our industry will tell you that the single, biggest telecommunications issue that businesses face today is the requirement for mobility. Mobility includes providing service for laptops, smartphones, and tablets for both staff and guests. This phenomenon is often referred to as BYOD, or Bring Your Own Device, and current studies show that the average employee now has 2.5 devices that need to be connected to your data network. All of that mobility equipment has to be dealt with by understanding whether it will connect well within your system, and whether you have enough bandwidth to provide the throughput for your mobile devices.

A simple example might be the guest vendor that arrives to do a presentation in your building. You will need to provide wireless access and you're probably going to want that wireless access segmented from the rest of your data network. You're going to need password controls, and you're going to need to understand how much bandwidth you're willing to provide. You also need to make sure that tight security is enforced. Even though guest access is segmented, it's important to understand your usage and resource allocation.

In addition to that, your staff will be using your data network with mobile devices. Their smartphones may be checking email when they're in your building. Their tablet devices might be doing certain tasks on your data network that used to always be done on the hardwired desktop computer that you also provided for that employee. So this mobility plan will require a level of management that you might not have considered before, and part of that is going to be security.

An essential role of security is to segment your data network, that is, secure your business databases from outside users and guest users on your wireless system. You need to have robust Wireless Access Points, firewalls, and data switches that enable this security. Beyond that, on the cellphone end, the smartphone end, there is a potential security risk in any employee cellphone device, whether you reimburse for it or not, or whether you provide it or not, and you may or may not be aware of this condition.

As an example, you might have a sales staff of five or six people who are responsible for, let's say, 100 or so clients in your company, and the majority of your voice communications with those clients and your sales staff might occur over cellphones or smartphones, and increasingly that's the way a lot of today's sales force works. As opposed to making a call from the office, they might be doing it from home or from the road on their cellphones.

So what's wrong with that? Potentially, nothing is wrong with it, except understanding that the client will be receiving the caller identification of your sales rep as opposed to your company. Is that important to you? Maybe, or maybe not. If you want to protect your brand and present a professional image to your client base, you might want an application that identifies the company name to the client even though the call comes from a salesperson via his cellphone or smartphone. Those applications are available, you need to know about them, and you probably should be considering implementing this technology.

Here's the downside risk of not doing it. If you have any turnover in your sales force, you might find yourself with the sales rep that goes to another company with your contact database on their smartphone, and clients that have never known any other number or possibly have never known any other number but the cellphone from that sales rep. That's a good way to lose some clients.

So what can you do about it? There are mobility applications that will allow you to manage those cellphones, wipe the database when an employee leaves: the contact database can actually be removed from the cellphone. The likelihood that your company caller ID that's been presented in your clients much greater with that application than without. This certainly needs to be considered.

Remote Workers

You're probably not much different than most organizations, SMBs and large enterprises, who are trying to take advantage of the employee expertise that might be available not just in the office, but from the home or from the road as well. To take advantage of this resource, connecting remote workers back to your company is something you need to know how to do, you need to know how to control it, and you need to find out the best way of accomplishing it.

Remote workers can be fixed in place, and may be either part time or full time employees that manage your call center and work from their homes or a small office. They might also be users that have an office in your building, but on certain days of the week would like to be able to work from home and would love to be fully connected back to the office. Many technologies enable that to happen, some more easily than others, some more secure than others. It's important that you work with a vendor who can help you design and implement a system that can enable your remote workers to be productive and secure. Enabling remote workers is an opportunity to take advantage of human capital that you have within your organization, and you need to make sure that you enable that to happen in an intelligent way.

To give you one example, we are working with a distributor that has a dozen or so offices throughout the state of California with a very experienced workforce, some of whom are getting close to retirement. One of the business choices that the business owner came up with was, "Well, we can retire these folks who are still very productive, but may not want to come to work 40 hours a week like they used to. Option A is that we'll retire them and train brand new employees, waiting for a few years before they come up to the speed of these experienced workers that we currently have in place. Or B, maybe what we'll do is offer these folks part time employment from their homes, taking advantage of their expertise and allowing them to be fully connected into our business, thereby saving ourselves the cost of full replacement of these employees one by one as these folks retire. At the same time, we'll enable them to slow down and enter into semi-retirement." The company went with Option B, and we learned that this option worked out really well. They were able to take advantage of these employees who are very happy to be engaged with a business that they've been working in their entire careers, and the company is hiring new people, but they're doing the hiring at a pace that makes sense, and in fact, getting some training help from their experienced staff as well. In this case, having a telecommunications system that enables remote worker capability obviously is the enabler here in your ecosystem. Without it, you won't be able to take advantage of that opportunity.

Call Centers | Contact Centers

Many smaller organizations will say, "Well, we don't have a call center. We don't have a boiler room. We don't have 20 people sitting in cubes with headsets on answering incoming calls." But our experience is that most organizations have at least two or three people at inside sales and maybe a handful of people in customer service that are truly small call centers. You may not be enabling them with the technology that's available. You may be doing not much more than answering incoming calls on a multi-button phone, and if Joe takes one, Mary takes the next, and if the call is for them, fine, and if it's not, they will transfer the call or take a message.

Most modern telephone systems offer almost free software that will enable you to handle incoming calls from your clients, prospects, and vendors better than you are now, and this functionality is available with premise-based or cloud-based systems. This functionality includes intelligent routing, call overflow, where if one group of people is busy, the system sends the call elsewhere as opposed to simply having the caller hang up or sending them to voicemail. You may be able to present information like your caller's time in queue or how many people are waiting in front of you, and maybe most importantly, you might be able to send the incoming call, based on the caller's number, to the right person in your organization the first time. In addition to that, the ability for the caller to request a callback is there as well.

Beyond that, call centers are moving into the web. Web interfaces can now be integrated into your call center. In fact, the front end of your call center might be your web page, your e-commerce page, and it might be enhanced by voice communications in the not too distant future. You're probably seeing some websites where you see a little chat window that pops up as soon as you spend more than a minute or two looking at a particular product, that's one small example. More sophisticated websites will also have a button for you to click on that will create a voice conversation, or give you a voice callback based on the product information that you needed to get from that website. This kind of capability is going to get a lot more seamless with the newer technologies, Web Real Time

Communications (WebRTC) being one of them. You need to understand that whatever you decide to do today in the way of your voice system needs to be assessed with a look to the future of a lot more sophisticated integration into customer relationship management/contact center/call center technology that's coming down the pipe.

Much of this capability is very well developed, very well fleshed out. And, it's not expensive. If you upgrade your system to any sort of modern VoIP system, you'll find most of those capabilities are there. Your telecom vendor can help you implement this capability.

An effective call center frequently includes Customer Relationship Management (CRM) integration into your incoming call center. It doesn't require a team of engineers and thousands of dollars of hardware and software to accomplish like it used to only a number of years ago. What we're talking about doing here is taking your database that you probably have for your clients already and hooking that into your incoming call center.

As an example, if you call into your bank, the person who answers the phone knows who you are and probably has a pretty good idea of what you're calling about, because when they answered the phone, there's a screen that popped up with your information on it, your account number, and so on. Now, they may ask some security questions to allow them to continue talking, but that information is there.

So that link between a database that you probably already have on your clients and your incoming call center can be hooked together pretty easily, and it can greatly enhance the productivity of the staff answering those calls in your company.

The implementation of effective call centers will be a key differentiator in the marketplace. The companies that grasp the technology first and design their systems around it will have a distinct competitive edge in the marketplace. We are seeing more and more customers using the web as a front end to buy products and services as opposed to in the past as simply being a way to conduct research. You need to understand how that works and how that's could be integrated into your particular business.

Wireless Network (WiFi)

It's rare to find a business today that has not installed wireless access points to enable wireless laptops, smartphones, and tablets to communicate within the organization. This is a fast-growing area, and it's one that requires some expertise to do well. The first priority is to secure your wireless access. You don't want it to be like the wireless access at Starbucks where just about anybody with a first-grade degree in hacking can be found snooping through your proprietary information.

Wireless systems have changed pretty dramatically in the last five or six years. Small businesses just a little while ago had nothing more than a very inexpensive wireless router perhaps connected to the internet allowing for the occasional employee with a laptop computer to have access to the internet.

That all has changed. A modern sophisticated small- and medium-sized business now may have as many wireless devices as they have hardwired devices on premise, and that includes not just laptop computers, but tablets, whether iPad or Android devices, and a wide variety of smartphones that your managers, employees, vendors, and clients are using almost continuously.

You're also going to want to differentiate who gets bandwidth and what they have access to in your system. Users with different access levels might include staff, guests, and perhaps even security personnel within your organization if you have that. For example, hospitality businesses frequently have all these access levels. There are a number of wifi systems that do that for you and that can be managed very easily, but you're going to probably need some help in selecting and implementing those systems.

Finally, you'll want to make sure that signal strength and reliability matches the needs of your users. You'll want to make sure that the wireless access points can deliver adequate signal strength, you'll want to make sure that any environmental factors are considered, and you'll want to be able to monitor usage and system outages. And remember, even though it is a wireless system, the wireless access points need to be wired with your structured cabling.

Video

Interestingly, video is an area of the ecosystem that has been the "hot new thing" for the last 30 years. It's never quite taken off, but we think it may soon. Video conferencing in the typical full conference room setting has not been widely adopted, and for good reason: it's expensive, it's cumbersome to set up and is basically point to point, and it requires that the users be in a specific location to take advantage of it.

The newer video conferencing systems are now available on the desktop, and even on smartphones and tablets, they're not as difficult to set up, and they don't require quite as much expense to provide the service.

So the increasing use of video conferencing is something you need to consider and you need to know how to get it enabled in your business. Video conferencing still has all the advantages have been touted in the past and it can cut down on travel, whether that travel is local or long distance or cross country or across the world. Video conferencing in the correct environment can be a money saver for an organization, and can help speed communications.

The other component of video is surveillance and security. Not the NSA kind, but maybe the simple stuff that allows you to see what's going on in your warehouse after hours, securing your egress and ingress and your company's front door and back door.

Video surveillance has now become IP enabled and video surveillance systems today are can be monitored from anywhere with a simple web browser. For example, we have video cameras set up in our organization that our key people have access to from anywhere basically to let us know what's going on in our facility.

The Cloud

All right, so what else could there possibly be in your telecom infrastructure? The new entrant is "the Cloud". You have all heard about it, and in fact, most of you are using the cloud in some area of your business today.

One of the things to understand about the cloud is that there are two kinds of cloud services. One is computing, which is asynchronous by nature, and the other is communications, such as voice and video, which is by necessity real time. The cloud handles computing applications really well, but has not yet perfected real-time communications.

There are some advantages to migrating some functions to the cloud:

- Experts maintain the hardware for you as opposed to your own IT staff being required to do that;
- Automatic updates for software enhancements when they come along as opposed to your onsite staff;
- Lowering of capital expenditures in some circumstances can be achieved by moving your application services to the cloud;
- Scalability of the services to accommodate nearly unlimited growth;

- Remote access to the services provided.

Cloud services cover much of the functionality we've been discussing, but it moves much of the equipment from your premises to somewhere else accessible by internet, and that could be a data center, it could be several data centers, or it could be in a carrier's location. Many of the services such as voice systems, virtual servers, application software such as Microsoft Office, your email exchange server, accounting applications, and many other applications can now be hosted in the cloud. A newer area of cloud service provisioning is the virtual desktop, where we're talking about removing that PC or workstation from under the desk and simply having a monitor with a thin client connection to the cloud and having all your software, Microsoft and otherwise, hosted in the cloud.

One example that we've come across recently: small startup technology firms are taking advantage of the relative ease and inexpensive nature of getting some of their R&D done on virtual servers that are hosted elsewhere, and once again, that can be in any number of data centers or any number of carriers. The attractive thing about it is that while they are paying for renting space and virtual servers, they are able to use freeware, such as Linux, to develop whatever application that they're working on. This enables small companies, and you might be one of them, to develop new applications at a very low cost. And it enables that to happen almost anywhere in the world because you're accessing these resources through the cloud. It turns out that you can convert from R&D to production pretty quickly, maybe buying paid for licenses on the operating system that you've been developing on, but keeping the work that you've done and the code that you've written on the virtual servers that you've been using. So that's an area that you might want to take a good look at.

Of course, cloud services come with cautions and challenges as well. In the case of cloud based phone systems, your organization will still need to have a structured cabling system in place to serve the endpoints, including phones, computers, printers, etc. And many times, the phones themselves will need to be purchased up front. In addition, selecting the right carrier and the right bandwidth product to support the cloud services becomes even more critical.

Most companies are already implementing some level of cloud services. For example, most small organizations are doing database backups in the cloud through some provider, such as Carbonite or MozyPro. It's a pretty straightforward thing to do, and it removes the risk of losing that data on-site, or having somebody forget to do the backup when they should. That's one small example.

Another example is that small and medium business users are often choosing not to maintain the costs and expertise required for a local email exchange server. Those services are provided in the cloud from literally scores of providers. It's something we would encourage small and medium sized organizations to consider.

Voice services also can be hosted in the cloud, but it isn't automatic that this makes sense for your organization. It's hard sometimes to get a high-quality, reasonably priced hosted voice application in the cloud. There are circumstances however when that might make sense, especially for small branch offices and remote workers.

There is one area of voice communications in the cloud, however, that we find might be a very promising application to consider, and that's call centers. It's also one of the fastest growing segments of cloud services, and we'll explain why. If you have ten people in your company sitting in cubes with headsets, expensive PCs or workstations, expensive connections to onsite servers and databases, handling dozens or hundreds of calls per day from your important incoming customer service calls or sales calls, you're aware that the cost of doing that is maybe close to $75,000 or $80,000 a year per user in total cost of provisioning. That's the salary, the burden of equipment, the connectivity, et cetera. Call centers in the cloud can enable you to have a professional organization handling your incoming call center for you, or enable you to have your own employees handle that incoming traffic from their homes, saving you some infrastructure costs and data systems costs as well. We're not talking about call centers in India or the Philippines, although they were the very first implementers of call center services in the cloud. Now, the capability has scaled down now to the point where even small businesses with only ten or so seats may find it very attractive economically to move some of that incoming call center traffic to the cloud.

Unified Communications

Another relatively recent development in the telecom ecosystem is something called UC or Unified Communications. Unified communications is an over-arching conceptual term. It's an attempt by our industry to combine many of the different kinds of communications into a single system or a single view for all forms of communication. For example, you could get an email message in your Exchange Outlook client that contains an MP3 of your voicemail, which you could then listen to and forward. UC can mean combining voice streams, voice communications, potentially video, video conferencing, messaging, non-real time messaging like email, social media, voicemail, IM chat, and something called presence.

Presence simply means the current state of anyone on your system in regards to their availability. If they're not in the office, they may be unavailable. If they're in the office and they're not on the phone, that presence might be called available. "Out to lunch", "in a meeting", "be back soon", "on the phone", are other instances of presence.

Is it important to know that? Yes, if you're working and collaborating with a team, it's a great idea to know the presence of everybody on that team so you don't waste time trying to communicate when you can see at a glance that that person might not be available, or when they might become available.

Presence can be very sophisticated depending on the system that you ultimately implement. It can give you a fine level of detail on not just the presence now, but the future availability of that employee, client, or vendor.

The idea of Unified Communications is that it's an enabler for collaboration. Equipping employees in your organization with a rich UC client can enable information transfer to happen quicker, more intelligently and from a single point of view as opposed to going to three different places to get the information: retrieving an email in Outlook, going into your phone to retrieve a voicemail and maybe asking Sally if Joe is in the office or not. All of that communication can be viewed in a single window on your smartphone or your computer.

So to recap Unified Communications, it's many things to many people, and it's different things to different manufacturers. This is an area where you're going to want to separate the sizzle from the steak. Some folks think they need to have it just because everybody is talking about it. Think about specifically what components of unified communications will make sense for your business, and engage your outside vendors, such as Team One Solutions, to help you with educating you about the opportunities for your business.

Support

Finally, your ecosystem, including all of the components that we've talked about above, requires support, whether that's your phone system, your cable infrastructure, your servers, your local area network, your mobile devices, your PCs, your video conferencing equipment, and more. Support for these components can come from many sources.

Many organizations have somebody, perhaps an IT guy, or a systems administrator, taking care of the local equipment, the premise servers, your PCs, the printers, the software updates. Many other organizations have gone to contracting a lot of that to IT-managed service providers. It's becoming very popular, and in some cases, reasonably inexpensive as well.

It's important to understand what your support looks like today. Do you have service contracts? Are you simply paying time and materials when something breaks? How does that affect your organization? Are you doing it as efficiently and as economically as you could?

In addition to the maintenance of your systems, an element of support that you need to consider is business continuity and disaster recovery. What sort of plans do you have for supporting your business in the event of something as simple as a power failure, which might require some uninterruptible power supplies to heal?

Or what are you doing with disaster planning? What happens if the telephone and data lines to your building get broken during a construction event? What do you next? Are you stuck with cellphones only, or have you prepared by setting up a forwarding mechanism with your carriers to allow those calls to go somewhere else or find another route?

In the event of a major disaster - earthquake, flood, hurricane - where your building may be completely out of service for some period of time, what plans have you put in place to continue the business? Do you have something set up that will allow your employees to work in another location, or remotely from their homes? Are you familiar with the enabling technologies to allow you to do that? Have you considered how manual or automatic that process might be?

Our company has set up disaster recovery plans for many of our organizations that we work with on a daily basis, and they can include things like having your important data and voice systems in a data center offsite or multiple data centers. This is an area where the cloud can provide real value and real help for business continuity in the event of a disaster.

A final aspect of support that we'll cover is regulatory compliance. The financial and the healthcare industries in particular have very specific and increasingly complex requirements for the kinds of communication security and archiving that are required. Recording and archiving of all kinds of messages are now required, not just of voice recordings, but also instant messages and emails, as well as the ability to recover those messages when required. This process doesn't have to be complicated and it doesn't have to be wildly expensive, but it needs careful and thoughtful implementation and support.

To get updates to this book and access to our videos that will show you how to grow your business with the strategies in this book, plus an invitation to interactive online livecasts to meet the author and his team, visit:

- http://os4.com/r/TEAM1, or
- text "telecom" and your email to 58885, or
- text your email address to (510) 574-7500, or
- scan this QR Code:

3 | Taking Your Telecom Inventory

We're at the point now where we need to start talking about getting an inventory of the telecommunications systems and applications that you have in your business.

So first of all, let's locate the system components and then understand the cost structure for those components and, importantly, let's understand the contract terms and possible early termination penalties associated with them as well.

We're doing all of this so that we can identify some of the potential challenges that your existing systems and components may have in allowing you to grow and win in your business, and perhaps some of the opportunities for doing just that by either tweaking, upgrading or replacing many of the components in your business.

Employee Profile

Let's start with some of the obvious stuff. How many employees do you have, and where are those employees located? It may sound like a simple thing, but it's important to know because each one of those employees is not only an asset, but every one of those employees needs to have some form of access to the communications and computing assets in your business.

Once you have your employee count, it's time to understand how those employees use your telecommunications systems. How many have wired phones at a desk with a computer? How many only have cell phones, such as delivery personnel or sales people? How many employees work from home, either part time or all the time? How many people do you have in call groups, such as customer support and sales? How many of your employees also have smartphones and tablets that they expect to connect to company resources when they are in the office?

Locations

The next step in taking your inventory is to identify your locations. Obviously, if you're a single location firm, it's pretty simple. But if you have more than one location, you need to know what they have in the form of assets, and how you're connecting those locations with other assets in your company. Are your locations close to each other, in the same city, region, or state, or are they scattered throughout the world?

Voice Systems

This may seem like an easy task because you've had a voice system ever since you've been in business, and most organization leaders are somewhat familiar with them. Here are the answers you need to have:

- Phone system manufacturer (Nortel, Avaya, Cisco, ATT, ROLM, Mitel, Intertel, Executone, etc.)
- Model of phone system, if different (e.g., Meridian, MCBX)
- Date system acquired

- Vendor currently providing phone system support
- Currently under maintenance contract? If yes, what are the response times, and when does the contract expire?
- # attendant consoles
- # phone type 1 (e.g. single line phone with no display)
- # phone type 2 (e.g., 2 line phone with display)
- # phone type 3
- # voicemail users, if any
- Auto-attendant?
- Call centers?
- Call recording?

This may seem a little pedestrian and you might be wondering why you need to know all this information. As we learned in an earlier chapter, voice systems have changed pretty dramatically in the last several years, and you may in fact have a phone system that's no longer supported by the manufacturer. It's important to know that. Even if your old phone system is still running and working well for you, it could present a downside risk to your operations if it should break or if it should need to grow, or if it cannot be enhanced to do some of the kinds of things that you determine are critical to your organization's success.

It is important to know which applications are running on your voice systems. One that everybody is familiar with, of course, is voicemail. But not all voicemails are created equally. Not all businesses have a voicemail system that allows enough storage capacity, ease of access, the ability to retrieve messages remotely, the ability to exchange messages with other people in your organization, whether they're onsite or not. If you have a voicemail system, how well is it working for you, and what challenges are you having?

From a high-level perspective, how does your company call flow work? Do you have an attendant who answers all the calls that come in from 8 to 5 and then transfers them to whoever is available? Or do you have an auto-attendant allowing the incoming party to decide which person or department he or she wants to talk to in the organization? Is this methodology working well for you?

Do you have a customer service department, or a sales department that's staffed with more than one person? Do you have separate numbers that go to an ACD (Automatic Call Distribution) group or groups? How is the existing system working for you, and what kind of challenges are you experiencing?

Finally, do you have call recording and retrieval? This may be necessary if your organization is in the financial or health care industry.

Data Systems

Moving on to data systems, it's a bit more complicated for most business managers to understand, but we're going to keep it at a higher level, and hopefully, not get too geeky. Fundamentally, your data systems boil down to the hardware you have connected, such as computers, servers, printers, and more, and the software applications you are running. Your hardware and your applications can be running locally in your facility, or they can be located offsite, or in the cloud. It's important to know what you have, and where you have it.

Let's discuss applications first. The kinds of applications that you are running are either going to be enabled or hindered by the quality of your data systems you have and the people running them. Common applications include:

- Operating systems (Windows, Mac, Linux/Unix)
- Email
- Accounting
- Customer Relationship Management (CRM)
- R&D
- Enterprise Resource Planning (ERP)
- Human Resources (HR)
- Point of Sale (POS)

It's very important to understand which versions of each application you are running, and where you are in the life-cycle of those software applications. For example, we have a couple of prospects who are still running Microsoft XP as the operating system on their PCs. It's been stable and reliable for them, but Microsoft terminated support in April, 2014. One of the serious downside risks of not upgrading those systems is that the organization will become much more vulnerable to getting hacked. The important question is whether your organization has the physical data systems in place to allow you to upgrade.

Now, let's get a handle on your hardware assets. The first and probably most obvious hardware asset is to understand how many computers your employees have, and where they are located. What operating system are they running? What are the challenges your organization is facing with the computers your staff is using?

The next area to consider is printers, scanners, and fax machines. Companies used to routinely supply printers to everyone who had a computer, but that model is being replaced with shared, networked printers. Most modern printers offer multiple functionality including copying, scanning and faxing. What kind of printers do you have? Where are they physically located? How many of them are standalone, and how many are networked?

Next, it's important to understand your server infrastructure. How many servers do you have, and where are they located? Are they onsite, offsite in a data center, or both? What are the biggest challenges you are having with respect to your server infrastructure?

Your firewall is one of the most critical components of your data systems. Be sure to understand what type of firewall you have, how expandable it is, and whether your IT staff has concerns about your firewall.

The cable infrastructure that you have in your building is what connects most everything that we've just talked about together. Your voice systems and your data systems are all connected via your cable infrastructure.

That cable infrastructure also needs to be inventoried. Is it enabling the kind of throughput that you need for your data workstations and servers? Is it going to enable you to take advantage of a VoIP system if you don't have one yet? And importantly, is it installed correctly, labeled correctly, enabling you to make changes and to grow your system with the least amount of interruption?

Many people view cable infrastructure as something you do once when you buy a building or move in to a new space and you don't ever think about it again. The reality is that if you're not connected correctly, everything else can easily fall apart. You can't have a connection to a printer if you don't have the appropriate connection to it.

You probably don't want your network service administrator spending half a day figuring out how to connect the new employees to new workstations. A professionally installed cable infrastructure system will make everybody's life easier and will provide a level of connectivity required to run a modern data systems and the applications running on them.

Carriers

Now, we need to consider how we connect all our devices to the outside world, which is through carriers. Depending on your operations, you may have one, two, or three carriers or more, one for telephone service, another one for internet service, and yet another one for cell phones.

Let's talk first about your voice carrier. Somewhere in a drawer is the 3- or 4- or 5-year contract that you signed with AT&T when you moved into your building. Somebody needs to pull that out and find out what you're paying, and whether you still have an obligation under that contract. You may find out that you want to take another look at every single carrier contract that you currently have and that you might want to switch carriers. But you can't do that if you don't know what you have right now. One of the disadvantages of current carrier contracts, whether for voice, cellphone, or internet access is that the regulatory bodies, both nationally and statewide, have enabled the carriers to sign you up to a contract that you will find very difficult to terminate before the end of the term. You will need to understand how much of your contract term you still have left, and what it could cost you if you determine you want to get out of it.

Here is the information you need to determine the current state of your voice carriers:

- Name of telco (ATT, Comcast, TelePacific, etc.)
- Contract terms: start date, end date, auto-renew date
- # analog trunks (including fax and alarm lines)
- # PRI trunks
- # T1 trunks, included bonded trunks, and DS3
- # SIP trunks
- # MPLS trunks
- Trunks supplied by copper or fiber or other medium?
- Monthly cost of telephony service

Next you'll want to inventory your internet service provider, or providers, if applicable. Go find that old contract, and get current billing statements from accounting and answer the following questions:

- Name of Internet Service Provider
- Start date:
- Term (in months)
- End date:
- Auto-Renewal date
- Service type
- Bandwidth description

Now you'll want to inventory your mobile phones, whether company provided or company paid for or some combination thereof. We've run into several companies who have told us that their cellphone costs surpassed all of their other carrier costs combined, so it's important you get a handle on this expense. It may be shocking to understand that you might not have a good handle on this expense, but that frequently happens in organizations if various departments pay for plans or reimbursements separately. In that case, the cellphone expense doesn't show up anywhere as a single line item.

Do you routinely provide management and executives with smartphones? Do you provide your sales staff with smartphones, and what about your delivery staff? Here is the information you need to get a handle on your mobile phone inventory.

- Mobile phone provider, if company provided (May or may not be the same telco listed above)
- # Management phones
- # Sales staff phones
- # Operations staff phones
- Monthly cost of company provided mobile phones
- # phones reimbursed by company
- Monthly cost of reimbursed mobile phone service

Wireless Systems

The next area is your wireless infrastructure. It used to be something pretty straightforward, just a little wireless router, probably that you paid less than $100 for and was only used occasionally for the guy with the laptop who came in to the office from a sales trip.

As we discussed earlier, most business are facing rapidly increasing demand for wireless services. The action to take now is to inventory your wireless network, preferably on a drawing of the company's facility. What wireless controllers do you have (if any), and how many wireless access points (APs) you have and where they are located. Where are your weak points in your ability to deliver wireless services in your organization? Are you getting complaints about speed, reliability, or weak signals? You probably are going to need more bandwidth than you currently have, and it also means that you're going to need to find out how you are managing that access.

Modern wireless systems will allow you to monitor, provide security, enable to segment the sort of wireless access you provide between staff, guests and vendors, and you can segment beyond that even to which staff have access to what components of your system.

Wireless systems today are connected not just to the internet, but they're also connected to your internal systems as well. So understanding what you have or don't have in the way of security, monitoring and control of wifi access is a very important component of your system that you need to understand.

Call Centers | Contact Centers

Now we'll touch on call centers. As you think through your organization, you may already have a well-identified call center, and you may even have a call center system that enables you to manage this function. If you do, it is important that you identify this, and note what is working well, and what the challenges are.

Even if you don't have formal call centers, you should take the effort to review your various departments to understand where establishing a more defined call center would be helpful. For example, do you have a sales department that picks up calls from a specified phone number? Do you have a service department, or a billing department that is a group of people that answer calls? If so, you essentially have call centers. Document how they currently work, and some of the challenges that those groups are facing. It is entirely likely that implementing call center technology could substantially benefit your company's top and bottom lines. How are these groups connected to the outside, and what communications methods are they using, such as phones, emails, chat, and video?

Some of the processes to document include whether you currently have a customer database or CRM system, and whether it is connected to, or integrated with, your voice system. Also, are all the members of these groups located in the same area, or are they spread out? Would it be advantageous to you to have personnel in these groups who are geographically remote from each other so you could provide service in more time zones? We have scores of clients that utilize remote customer service representatives working out of their homes to answer incoming calls.

The action to take here is to document where in your organization you have call centers, how those systems currently work, and what challenges and opportunities you are currently facing with those call centers.

Video Services

Now it's important to understand the video services your organization employs. These services can be broken into video conferencing and video security.

There are two kinds of video conferencing, fixed video conferencing, typically in a specialized conference room, and individual desktop video conferencing, which is becoming a much more popular. How are you using these systems, and what challenges are you experiencing with their use?

The other video service is security and surveillance. Outside video security is sometimes provided by your landlord or it's something that you provide in your business if you have your own building. Do you have just a camera and a monitor somewhere in your office? Do you also have the ability to record video and retrieve it. The necessity for connectivity to that security system is becoming increasingly important. IP or Internet Protocol video surveillance systems are now becoming increasingly more popular for the reason that they can be monitored from anywhere. Does your current system, if you have one, have this capability? We have one in our business, and it enables us to see what's going on inside and outside of our building from any browser.

Cloud Services

Many small- and medium-sized businesses claim that they have not adopted the cloud and don't believe that they're using any cloud services currently. I would argue that we would be hard pressed to find any organization almost anywhere in the country that's not using cloud services to some degree. It's kind of a trick question, but if you have a smartphone and you have one application on it that has anything to do with your business, then you're in the cloud already. Here are some of the many cloud based services you might have:

- Data backup and synchronization
- File sharing
- Email
- CRM (Salesforce.com for example)
- ERP
- Accounting
- Project Management
- Desktop application software (such as Microsoft 365)
- Telephone services

Do the inventory with the understanding that you probably don't have all of those components, but find out how much of it you actually do have. Why do you need to know? You may want to start migrating more of your data services into the cloud, and you can't do that if you don't know what you're using now and how much you might want to use in the future.

Be sure to document problems you are currently having with any of these types of applications, or write down other challenges that your organization is facing that might have a cloud-based service.

Support Structure

All of the above - cloud services, video, call centers, wifi, data systems, voice systems, applications - require support of some kind or another. You are probably doing a little of both in-house support, whether that's a CIO, an IT manager, or network administrators and outside contractors. What is the mix, who supports which systems, and approximately what are you paying for those support services?

We find that the average small and medium business now has cut back on IT staff and enhanced it with the use of outside subcontractors, whether that's fully managed service providers that take care of everything from upgrading your software and your workstations and your servers, fixing printer problems when they occur, to simply ad hoc time and material and IT experts that come in when you need some help.

Understanding the cost of your support systems, whether that's in-house staff or outside contractors or managed services or some combination of all of the above is very important. You may be spending more than you should. You may be spending less than you should, and we suggest that because without the correct amount of support, all of the systems that we just reviewed are not going to be optimized, and will not to be as efficient as they could be, to make sure that your business is growing and competing as well as it could.

To get updates to this book and access to our videos that will show you how to grow your business with the strategies in this book, plus an invitation to interactive online livecasts to meet the author and his team, visit:

- http://os4.com/r/TEAM1, or
- text "telecom" and your email to 58885, or
- text your email address to (510) 574-7500, or
- scan this QR Code:

4 | Your Business Plan

Many of the strategies that will affect what you do with your communications equipment systems will be dependent upon what your plans are for your business as a whole.

Growth or Consolidation

The very first question: is your business in the growth mode, or are you consolidating? These are the key drivers for what you might want to do with your communications systems. As an example, if you are in the growth mode, you know you're going to need more bandwidth, and you might therefore want to be hesitant about re-upping long-term contracts with your current vendors. You might need more resources or different services than you currently have under your existing contracts.

Here is one small example. If you have plans for moving your existing location, you want to make sure that your new location offers the appropriate amount of telecommunication services, particularly internet bandwidth that you might need. That wasn't as important a consideration five or six years ago, but we run into many clients now that are requiring five to ten and even more times the amount of bandwidth that they used in their old facilities, and you need to know whether or not that's available when you move this new office park, to the new industrial building or wherever it happens to be. You need an expert to help you determine that.

Are you going to be growing through acquisition? This is a very disruptive event for many companies and their communications plans and systems. You might have what you feel to be an ideal computing and communications environment right now, but what happens if you acquire a company approximately your size that has totally disparate manufacturers, different systems, different IT staff, et cetera? What happens when you try to meld those two together? It's something to think about, and it's an area where you might need some outside help in blending the two organizations, and not just from the standpoint of personnel, but systems as well.

Sometimes there are wonderful economies of scale that you can gain through acquisition. Sometimes there is an opportunity for chaos if it's not done correctly.

Physical Locations

Multi-location or single is kind of basic, but those organization that have only a single location will probably find it much easier to develop a communications plan for the future than those organizations that have multiple locations. It's kind of obvious, but it needs to be stated.

Networking between locations and how you would accomplish that will be an important element of how you run your business. The methods for connecting multiple locations are varied, and you need to understand what they are and which ones make the most sense for you.

As a simple example, if you only had two locations and one was in downtown San Francisco, and the other was in Oakland, traditionally, you might not have done much more than getting a point to point circuit between the two locations to handle your voice and data traffic between the two.

Now, you've got many other options including straight internet connections and simply connecting the two sites via a VPN connection for voice and data, or maybe something a bit more sophisticated like an MPLS circuit that will allow you to not just have multiple data streams between the two points, but the ability to apply quality of service to those different streams. In this example, voice gets priority over that circuit and data comes in second because it's not real time. These technologies are available to everyone but not every business will find all of them appropriate. You should have an expert to help you.

Finally in that area of connecting multiple locations, your plan might include cloud services. Instead of your company managing the networking between your locations, you might simply hire a cloud service provider to manage that for you. Once again, the ability to develop a plan that's specific to your needs obviously is critically important.

Remote and Mobile Workers

One of the most widespread business trends during the last decade has been the proliferation of remote and mobile workers. What is your plan for remote workers? Remote workers can be full time, part time, and they can also be call center and/or customer relationship people who work out of their homes. The ability to include this functionality into your communications plan is important, as it may affect which system and system options you choose to implement. There are many ways to skin that cat. You can simply have a telephone line and an internet connection to connect your remote workers, or you might extend the office capabilities completely to the remote worker via an MPLS pipe, a VPN connection, requiring the right kind of carrier services and the right kind of endpoint equipment.

In some cases, the remote worker might be a physician, and you might need to provide video capabilities in addition to simply voice and data. If so, you need to have that in your plan.

Another area that most organizations have to deal with is the mobile worker, whether you've got 5,000 employees or 5. Mobile workers may include everyone in your organization, from the CEO to sales staff, to admin assistants. Anyone who uses a laptop, smartphone, or tablet and expects wireless access to company resources is a mobile worker. Supplying this capability is not free, and it's something that you have to plan for.

If you do have mobile workers using mobile devices, making sure that their communication is secure and not open to hacking is critical to securing your important business intellectual property. It also touches the area of bandwidth when those mobile workers arrive at the office. Is there enough internet bandwidth available to provide the level of service you want to those mobile devices that you're providing?

Customer Support Plan

Everything we've reviewed up to this point has been focused on providing communications services within your facilities. Let's move on now to your clients and prospects and how you are planning to support them. Are you now connecting in a very traditional manner with simple voice and email communications? As you are probably aware, these traditional methods of communicating with your client base and your vendors are changing rapidly, and you need to plan for it. In addition to voice, email, and snail mail communications with your clients and vendors, you are probably going to use some level of online communications, whether as simple as a list of your services on your website that are available to your clients, or whether it's something more sophisticated, including electronic ordering and fulfillment of products and services via your website.

This is the subject of customer relationship management (CRM), and it is a complex topic. The way you communicate, the way you acquire clients, the way you service clients that you currently have and the way you find new ones typically will involve a number of different communications technologies and methodologies. It might be voice with IVR (Interactive Voice Response), it might be chat, it might be WebRTC (Real Time Communications). You will probably want to plan on a contact center of some sort, and that contact center might be something as simple as three people in the customer service department in a hunt group properly handling incoming calls and service calls, or it might be something very much more sophisticated than that, depending on the volume of business you're doing. You should probably plan on integrating your client communications with your client and prospect databases in order to provide the highest and most efficient level of support. That in turn will lead to lower costs and higher revenue.

So you need a plan, and you need to understand what's available. You need to understand whether your current methodology is competitive today and in the near future, or whether you need to explore some of the newer technologies that are available. We recommend that you seek the help of an expert to assess what is right for your business.

Security

The subject of security is an increasingly important topic. The more you reach out to your clients, your vendors, and your employees via the web and mobile devices, the more important security becomes. It's in the news every single day of the week, whether we're hacking cellphones in Sochi or stealing 100 million credit card users' personal data from Target, or being exposed by the Heartbleed attack on "secure" websites, it's happening all the time and you need to protect your important business intellectual property by having the appropriate security systems and policies.

It touches on a lot of areas. It can be something as simple as the security camera at your front door, or something as sophisticated as a remotely monitored firewall system that enables you to manage not just internet access, but Wi-Fi access within your building, denial of service preventions on your website, and more. It's not only software security, but also physical security. You may want to have your voice and data servers in a locked room with a security camera.

Security **within** your company is a vitally important concern. Do you know or care what your employees are doing online? Is it all work related, or is it Facebook, or maybe something worse like sharing sensitive company information or visiting sites that might be inappropriate?

These concerns apply to voice and text communications as well as web activity.

The good news is that there are many tools available to enable you to secure and monitor your internal communications systems. You just need to add them to your overall strategic plan.

The implementation and strengthening of security needs to be in your plan and it's not just the single item that it might have been five years ago. You need to tailor your security plan to all of the rest of your computing and communications elements in your business. This is also an area where we advise the judicious use of experts.

Regulations

More and more businesses are subject to regulatory requirements. If you're in the healthcare field, you are increasingly required to provide electronic medical records and to comply with the HIPAA requirements. If you're in the financial industry, you've got a whole series of regulatory compliance requirements depending on what segment of the financial industry you happen to be in.

All of those regulations touch your computing and communications ecosystem, and they have to be accounted for. One simple example might be the requirement to record patient and/or client calls in both the healthcare and the financial industries. Not just to record them, but to have the ability to store them for some extended period of time and then to be able to retrieve the important information from those recordings in a timely fashion.

This is an area that most businesses did not have to worry about five or ten years ago. Today, many more, even small and medium sized businesses have to comply with new laws and regulations that cost real money.

Business Continuity and Disaster Recovery

The important question for you to answer is: "How critical is it that your business continues to operate even after a significant event, and what this is worth to you?" If you have the kind of business whose computing and communications systems need to be up and running five to seven days a week every week of every year or else people, or maybe your business, dies, then you need to have some level of business continuity and/or disaster recovery plan.

There is no one plan that fits all organizations. It depends on what kind of business you have, and the value of staying open during a disaster versus the cost of providing a back-up plan, and what the probability is that a significant event will even occur.

There are myriad ways of providing for business continuity and disaster recovery. There is no one single element that will provide protection in the event of a disaster. Power, server, and carrier redundancy, are just a few elements to be considered in developing a recovery plan. As important are personnel resource and asset location planning. Cloud services, data center backups, and alternate carriers and transmission media should be considered as well.

Make sure you create, and implement, a Disaster Recovery plan that is tailored to your operations.

To get updates to this book and access to our videos that will show you how to grow your business with the strategies in this book, plus an invitation to interactive online livecasts to meet the author and his team, visit:

- http://os4.com/r/TEAM1, or
- text "telecom" and your email to 58885, or
- text your email address to (510) 574-7500, or
- scan this QR Code:

5 | Select the Technologies

Up to this point in the book, we spent a lot of time learning about the telecommunications landscape, inventorying what telecommunications systems you have, and articulating where your organization is headed. Now, we're going to move on to practical advice about selecting the specific technologies you need to meet your goals.

Selection Team

Let's start with identifying who is going to get involved in putting this plan together, turning it from a document into reality. This is critical to the success of the plan as a whole. You have to have ownership for the project, and you need to figure out which stakeholders ought to be on the team that's going to be involved in making any changes in your systems.

Internal Team

Obviously, you want your ownership team: yourself, partners, whoever has got the biggest skin in the game for your company to be involved. Your IT department, if you have one, clearly should be part of the team. Don't ignore your sales and support staff. Revenue comes in the front door, and your systems, both communications and computing, should accommodate the needs of sales and marketing, and your support staff.

Resellers

Now get to work on selecting who's going to help you outside of your organization. There are many places to get the information that you need, the products that you need, and the services that you need in order to implement your plan. The easy place to start for information obviously is the internet. We work with clients all the time who have convinced themselves that they have come up with the right solution set, the right vendors, the right products, and the right system by spending a couple of days doing Google searches. We don't claim that you can't get some very valuable information that way, but it tends to be not very well vetted and it may not be precisely what it appears to be on the web pages that you've discovered.

As part of your selection plan, your internal team is going to have to get some help, and that help could come from any number of outside vendors. There are full service integrators and consultants who can help you in both design and implementation. You need to find out who they are, how they operate, who the best companies are in the field, who you need to avoid, and who you might want to work with.

You will quickly discover that in addition to full service integrators, in other words, those companies that design the systems, install the systems and maintain them, there's a whole other subset of providers, equipment brokers and gray market operators who can provide you with computing and communications equipment that will cost you less than if you bought it new from an authorized reseller. Every once in a great while, if it's commodity product, you might want to take a look at it, but for anything sophisticated, anything that's key to the success of your business, you probably want to avoid that.

By the way, when we say avoid that, it may not be as simple as you think. If you were to ask a Cisco reseller with a website that looks like a million dollars if his equipment is new and supportable, the answer is going to be "yes", whether or not that company is an authorized reseller. So you have to be a little savvy and dig a little deeper to make sure you're getting what you need.

There are also equipment brokers. This is the classification of business people that we recommend that you avoid. A broker is kind of a guy that knows where you can get stuff, will help you find it cheap, but will take little or no responsibility for the ultimate usability, reliability, or maintainability of what you've purchased.

Manufacturers

If you're considering replacing, enhancing, or upgrading either your communications or computing systems, a good place to start is with the manufacturers themselves. All the major manufacturers, like HP and Cisco on the computing side and Avaya, NEC, Mitel, ShoreTel, and Zultys on the voice side, have pretty good websites that will give you access to lots of information. It may not be easy to sort through, but the information will probably be there, so may be of some value to you.

As a small to medium sized organization, you're going to find that, with very few exceptions, almost none of the manufacturers will deal with you directly. There are manufacturer relationships with large enterprises that are direct, but, by and large, the channel (we call it the channel, the distribution channel) consisting of resellers, integrators and VARs, is how you will get your products and service.

Carriers

Another set of outside vendors that you're going to need to explore are your carriers, both voice and data carriers. There is an expanding product set that these carriers offer, from the analog line that you use for your fax machine to fiber-optic SIP trunking and high-speed bandwidth delivered in any number of new ways by multiple carriers. The carrier business is becoming more complicated than it used to be because it's not as much of a commodity business as it was. Twenty years ago if you needed five phone lines you would probably contact with AT&T or Verizon or your local rural carrier if you happen to be in a non-metropolitan area, and that would be the end of it.

If you needed an internet access ten years ago, you might go to somebody like Cogent and get a DSL line, and that's about as complicated as it got. What's makes it more complicated, more interesting, and potentially more valuable to you today is that carriers are now providing not just the pipe into your building to carry the bits and bytes and the voice conversations, but they are also providing some cloud services.

Almost all carriers today will offer you not just the voice and data communications pipes, but also some space in their own data centers where you can house your own servers or run your applications on their servers. In other words, the very carriers that used to provide only commodity services in the past are offering a whole wide variety of cloud services for every type of computing and voice needs you can possibly imagine.

Additionally, many carriers are now offering **managed** voice and data circuits using a technology called MPLS (multi- protocol label switching) that enable business of all sizes to network two or more of their locations in a way that was not possible just a few years ago. This technology provides a level of voice, data, and video (if needed) transmission quality at a price point much, much lower than earlier point-to-point technologies.

All of this makes it more complicated, and important for you to choose the right carrier. It means that the conversations that you have with the carriers are going to be more extensive than just how many voice lines can I get at what price, and what the long distance rates are. Rather than having multiple conversations with multiple carriers, you may want to delegate the evaluation and selection process to a trusted full-service integrator.

Selection Process

Finally, you're going to need to come up with a selection process. First, select the people on your team that should be involved, then review the vendors – full-service integrators, consultants, manufacturers, and carriers - that could likely provide services to you.

When you go about selecting a manufacturer, sometimes it seems easy. It may be a brand name that you've seen for years. They advertise on TV. For example, Cisco is kind of an easy one to come up with, but you need to know whether or not that particular manufacturer, even though the brand maybe recognizable, is appropriate for what you're trying to do in your business.

There is a value in reducing the number of vendors that you're going to be dealing with. It's easy to get distracted by conflicting claims, conflicting product sets, multiple points of view about how to get to the end game. You're going to want to get that down to a manageable number of choices.

In every instance, we recommend strongly to you that you only consider factory-authorized vendors. So if you do select, let's say, Cisco as a product set, make sure that in your selection process, you're only talking to resellers that are factory authorized by Cisco. This is a pretty straightforward and simple thing to verify, but not everybody does it.

You don't necessarily have to take the VAR or the integrator or the consultant's word for it. We suggest that you go to the manufacturer's site and check them out. Every manufacturer has a partner site that will tell you if the party you're talking to is authorized, and what level of expertise that particular vendor has on the product set. It's important to have a match there obviously.

You're going to want to work with people who have broad and deep experience. It sounds like a simple thing to say, but you can't always judge a vendor by his website or one or two references. You will want to be sure that you're doing business with an organization that has been in business for a number of years, and a number of years in the technology that you're looking at. You'll also want to know if they located where you are and the kind of support organization that they have to back up what they are designing and selling for you.

Make sure your value-added reseller is a company that takes the time to understand how you do business, what applications and what business processes are most important to your business, and then to helps you design the systems around your needs. That takes a vendor who has more than technical capability, more than just an understanding of how the technology works, but someone who will help you achieve your business goals. Clearly, not every vendor is going to have that capability.

References are key. You're probably going to want to find some references on your own in addition to those handpicked references that any vendor will be happy to send you. Not to say that they aren't valuable, but if you can't find references on the company's website that you can check independently, then you might pause for a moment to figure out whether or not that's going to be a viable partner for you.

A company's web presence is important. Make sure your potential vendor has taken the trouble to design and offer a website that will give you not just the background on the company, but the breadth of services that they offer, the certifications that they have, and the partners that they do business with. It's a pretty good first pass way of deciding who you want to talk to. Whether it's a consultant, a carrier, or an integrator that's going to put all the pieces together for you, it will tell you a lot about the company.

Decision Timeline

Next, it is important to assess the financial and business considerations to help you decide when to push the button to start the project. We recommend that you perform a financial ROI about your particular situation. Every organization is different. You may have old systems that are working. They haven't fallen apart yet. But are you convinced at this point that maybe you could be doing better? Could you be increasing revenue, or could you be enhancing productivity if you made the change? Estimate the value of those changes, and that will help you decide when to upgrade your system.

Do you have a system that's end of life/end of service with the manufacturer? We like to start here because the downside risk of losing a voice communication system that's not supportable can be enormous. Being without voice communications, except perhaps your cellphone, for any length of time cannot just cost revenue to your business, but might really negatively impact the perception that your clients have about your company, so that's a main consideration, and you need to throw that into the mix when deciding whether is it time to upgrade or not. What would be the consequences if your customer database was hacked because you didn't update your equipment?

You will find that most voice manufacturers have a program to transition you from your old legacy equipment to whatever it is that they want to sell you. Understand what those programs are, take advantage of them if you it makes sense for your organization.

Voice Technology Selection

There are multiple variables you need to consider in choosing the right voice technology for your organization. The two most important considerations are whether to go with 100% VoIP or a hybrid system and whether to consider the cloud, or hosted voice. Some of the determinants is this decision include whether your company has, or is going to have multiple locations, the extent to which your organization will have mobile and remote workers, whether certain UC functionality could add value to your business, and what the growth or consolidation rates are for your business.

VoIP or hybrid?

As we discussed in Chapter 2, there are some limited situations where you may not want or need to adopt a fully VoIP system. Do you currently have a facility that doesn't have any Cat 5 or 6 cabling, and the cost of installing that cabling would be prohibitive? Are you basically fine with the digital phones you currently have, but you want to take advantage of the cost effectiveness of SIP trunking? Then, you may want a hybrid solution from your existing PBX manufacturer, such as Avaya or NEC. If these considerations aren't applicable to you, it will probably be more advantageous for you to adopt a 100% VoIP solution.

Multiple locations?

If your organization has, or is going to have, multiple locations, then a VoIP system is almost certainly going to be compelling. Be sure that the manufacturer you select has an architecture that makes it easy and relatively inexpensive to add locations, and that the value-added reseller you choose has developed expertise in networking many multi-location systems for its customers. At Team One Solutions, we have scores of clients for whom we've implemented networked VoIP systems, regionally, nationally, and internationally.

Remote workers?

To what extent are remote workers going to be important to your business over the next several years? We've not met any small or medium-sized businesses in the last several years that don't have at least one remote or home worker. That needs to be addressed in your system. Most systems will offer a method for connecting your remote and home workers, some more easily than others. You need to understand how each vendor accomplishes this. Some systems allow remote workers to be provisioned quickly, securely, and inexpensively, utilizing technologies like NAT traversal.

There are many other systems that require expensive VPN hardware and/or software that may be difficult and time consuming to provision remote workers.

Mobility and BYOD

If your Business Plan from Chapter 4 is like most, you're going to see a trend of workers using their laptops, smartphones, and tablets for communications. Be sure that the voice system you select has a robust way of supporting these users, including easy-to-use apps. Ask your value-added reseller to review mobility and BYOD support in not only the voice technology proposal, but also the WiFi, security, and carrier proposals.

Unified Communications

If your Business Plan calls for greater levels of collaboration and accelerated speed of communications, you will likely want to implement at least some UC capability for some of your staff. Features like presence, voice, video and IM collaboration may be available. You need to understand clearly what UC capabilities come standard with the systems you are reviewing, and how additional UC capabilities get implemented. Is it a matter of software licensing, or is additional hardware also required? What are the costs to add UC features?

Messaging

Most every type of business messaging including real-time voice, voicemail, chat, IM and video are available on the best of today's communications system platforms, and can be integrated with many email platforms as well. Further, some systems will offer recording, storage, and retrieval of every one of these messaging formats. This capability is becoming more necessary for businesses of all sizes and stripes, not just for meeting regulatory requirements, but for improving business processes as well. As with most components of your voice technology selection, you'll want an expert guide to help you find and select those that make the most sense for your business.

Hosted vs CPE

In today's telecom market, this is the **big** decision. And it will probably be the most confusing, financially impactful, and potentially the most business affecting (good or bad) telecom decision that most small and medium businesses will make. A massive marketing effort is being devoted to persuading businesses to adopt hosted voice, to move to your communications to the cloud. After all, everything else has or soon will be in the cloud. Data storage, computing resources, software, music, gaming, photos, social media, movies, tax returns, banking, even your child's application to college, and so much more is "in the cloud".

Hold on. Voice is different. It's real time communications. It behaves differently, and has different requirements for achieving quality transmission than most other forms of data. Voice servers in the cloud do not share many of the benefits and economies of scale that other hosted applications have to offer. That is why, at this stage of development we believe that hosted voice makes sense for only a small range of organizations, and for the most part, CPE (customer premise equipment) will provide the best long-term value.

Remember when considering a hosted solution, you will still need to invest in structured cabling, including PoE switches, and you will still need to purchase phones, although this latter expense can sometimes be built into the monthly per-seat rate. In addition, you will still have to invest in secure firewalls and routers, and you will need to provide adequate bandwidth. Some hosted providers will rely on you to "Bring Your Own Bandwidth" (BYOB), while many carriers who provide bandwidth are now also providing hosted solutions.

The perpetual rental, per-seat pricing for hosted voice systems rarely will compare favorably with CPE systems., especially after you add in the fixed costs for infrastructure and handsets. The hosted providers will make the CAPEX vs OPEX argument, but equipment lease rates are at near historic lows now so that most CPE systems can be leased at a far lower monthly cost that hosted systems. The other argument to consider is the life expectancy of telecom systems. If they become obsolete in a three year period like PC's, servers and other data equipment does, then you might not want to own. This argument doesn't hold much water however. Your current legacy phone system may have been serving your business for 10, 15, or even 20 years. And the new voice systems are now software-centric rather than hardware-centric. This will allow you can easily upgrade CPE systems to take advantage of new technologies as they evolve.

Traditionally, the biggest issue with hosted voice has been voice quality. Skype, Vonage, and other providers that utilize the public internet have well-documented quality issues that have prevented their penetration into the business enterprise market. Newer, business-grade hosted services are now available and they offer higher quality managed circuits to overcome this issue, but, as you can imagine, that quality comes at higher cost.

Another, very important, consideration in choosing Hosted vs CPE is flexibility and customization. Businesses have become used to and dependent on the ability of their CPE voice systems to be highly customized to suit their individual business needs. Call flows, IVR, ACD, sophisticated auto-attendant "trees" are easily developed and configured on modern CPE systems, and importantly can be changed quickly and inexpensively. You will sacrifice a lot of that customization, feature richness, and agility with almost all hosted voice systems. The reason is simple—a single hosted soft-switch might serve hundreds or even thousands of end user companies. It is technically and economically unfeasible to offer anything other than very basic feature and configuration changes to individual hosted clients. Hosted voice today is a one, or at best, a very few, sizes fits all offering.

In general, we find that hosted solutions make the most sense when an organization is anticipating very rapid growth or consolidation, and can negotiate a short contract term. The other case where hosted makes sense is when the organization has multiple locations spread throughout a geographic area, especially if many of them are smaller offices serving, say, 1-25 employees.

When conducting the evaluation, it is important to start with getting an apples-to-apples comparison, which can be done pretty easily as long as you've got the right partner to help you step through it. Your provider for either solution is going to be extremely important, and many value-added resellers, like Team One Solutions, offer both hosted and CPE solutions.

The CPE providers are pretty well known. Most of them have been in the business for many years, and include NEC, Avaya, Cisco, Shoretel, Mitel, and Zultys. When you go to the cloud, it's a bit different. In the Bay Area, there are probably 25 or 30 cloud hosted VoIP providers, and they range anywhere from the $19 a seat/mo, "8 x 8" or RingCentral system which requires you to provide your own bandwidth, up to a very sophisticated soft switch-provided and managed connection to the provider's data center that might cost upwards of $50/mo. per seat.

Security

Every time you go off premise, you need to be secure, so some consideration for firewalls and VPNs that will secure your voice communications between Points A and B, are very important, and also whatever sort of WAN (Wide Area Network) hardware and software is required to make a quality connection between multiple locations is something else that you need to consider when putting your infrastructure in place.

Finally, it should be obvious that this decision will require expert guidance and due diligence to get right.

Training

Training is a very important component of a telecom system implementation, and you want to verify that the value-added reseller has a process in place to train not only the system admins, but also everybody in the organization who will be using the system. Don't discount the importance of having a very specific, well fleshed out, repeatable training process. By repeatable, we mean you're probably going to train everybody on how to use the system on Day 1 or the week after, but you're going to have employee turnover, you're going to expand, you're going to have new staff that never used that system before, so you need a plan in place that can repeat that training over and over again without reinventing the wheel. That may be anything from hard copy documentation to training videos that you've got resident on HR server, and anything in between. The best vendors will help you design training materials like that, that it will not only make your initial implementation a success, but it will keep it that way as you add new employees.

911

Not every VoIP system and not every cloud-based VoIP system has 911 capability that you may be legally required to have, or that you may simply want to have. It is a complex area of consideration, but the right vendor will help you make sure that you've got 911 covered for your facilities, whether it's your main office or your branch offices or your remote workers.

Call Center | Contact Center

Call centers usually exist in conjunction with your voice systems, but they can also exist as a separate entity. In many businesses, it is the front end of the revenue stream, and therefore an area that you should take particular time and attention to. You should ensure that you are optimizing the functionality of your customer contact center and your investment in it. This applies to people and systems. Frequently, this is an area that will earn the lion's share of any upgrade or system replacement.

The good news with call center technology is that manufacturers have been racing to provide call center functionality to the SMB market that used to only be available to large enterprises, and it is now reasonably priced and much easier to implement.

Modern CRM functionality now offers not just super-efficient call flows, skills-based routing, and reporting packages. Even small business versions come equipped with call queuing depth, wait time announcements, supervisor monitoring, and client database integrations. Would it make sense to integrate your call centers with your website? These are areas where your value-added reseller can educate you about the opportunities.

Data Networking Selection

Let's move on to your data networking plan, which may be intertwined with your voice system.

Structured Cabling

The first area to consider is your structured cabling. It's kind of a technical area, but obviously, before you do anything in the way of upgrading or adding or installing a new cable infrastructure, you're going to need a contractor that understands precisely what you might need. You should look for a contractor with the C7 license in the State of California. That's somebody who's authorized to install low-voltage devices and cabling and who will be able to help you to make sure it gets installed correctly.

If you're electing to stay with analog or TDM phones in a hybrid system, you may be able to reuse existing twisted pair copper wires. If you've selected a VoIP system, you'll need a minimum of Cat5 cable to support those phones. Most VoIP phones can share a single cable with your computer, but be sure to know your current and future bandwidth requirements to your workstations. If you require 1Gig to the desktop, make sure you either get VoIP phones that can handle that speed, or run 2 Cat5e or better cables to each desktop.

Fiber optic cable in most cases will be required for both data and VoIP connections over 300 feet. There are considerations for running fiber that are distinct from copper. The cost, the connectors, and the interfaces with your LAN switches are some issues to be aware of. Most importantly, be sure that your vendor has experience with designing and installing fiber media.

There are some code and environmental considerations that you have to be aware of, particularly if your business is in a metropolitan area like San Francisco, Oakland, or San Jose. There are specific code requirements that apply equally to new construction and to remodeled facilities.

Here's a good example of what you might be faced with that you may never have prepared yourself for. You've just leased 5,000 square feet of new office space in downtown San Francisco. The building looks good. It's the right size, the right location, the right configuration. Now, it's time to hook up your local area network, so you hire a cable contractor to come in and start running Cat 5 or Cat 6 or whatever it is you chose, and you found out that the cable runs have to be placed above the drop ceiling, and this typically is what will happen in most modern office buildings.

But when you open up that ceiling, you find out that the last tenant has left thousands and thousands of feet of cabling that they used on their network before they left. Be aware that all of that cable has to be removed, and there may, in fact, be a building inspector that comes by to make sure you remove all the unused cabling. This can be an expensive and unanticipated cost.

The other consideration here is plenum or non-plenum-rated cabling. Most licensed cable contractors will recommend plenum-rated cabling, and what that simply means is that there is a special coating on the outside of the cable that retaards ignition in case of a fire, and it prevents the emission of noxious gases. If there's ever any doubt as to whether or not your ceiling is plenum or not, and that simply means that the cold air return is going above the ceiling as opposed through ductwork, go for the plenum rated cable.

So, as you can see, even this relatively static and straightforward communication system component has its complexities and requirements that can't be overlooked.

Data Network Components

Your data network connects your servers, computers, including laptops and desktop stations, your VoIP system, network printers and fax machines, wireless APs, and networked video devices. Sizing the network component and their technical requirement is critical to creating an optimum telecom system.

This is where you should rely on your IT experts, who could be in-house, or specialized consultants, or it could be your value-added reseller. It's especially important to spec out your data switches with respect to the number of ports, throughput, power, security, and QoS. The scalability and the manageability of data switches varies widely both in cost and functionality. The $150 unmanaged switch from yesterday will probably not work well for you in the future.

With respect to firewalls, we're finding that even in the smaller end of the SMB market, firewalls have become a much more important consideration. Business have become subject to an ever increasing multitude of security breaches of all kinds, whether it's something as simple as somebody hacking into your VoIP phone systems and making unauthorized calls to the rest of the world, creating denial of service attacks on your website, or something as serious as hackers being able to get into your data network and start mining your client database. You need to have a high quality firewall, and you need to have somebody that understands firewalls to select and configure the appropriate levels of security that you need to run your business securely. So pay attention to it. It's not something you buy once and forget. You may need to reconfigure your firewalls from time to time based on your changing business environment, the types of connections you're making to the outside world, the types of vendors that you're connecting to, the types of clients that you're allowing access to some part of your internal systems.

The exit point of your local data network is typically a router. The router basically is a device that makes routing decisions about the best path for data streams to take between network segments. Your business LAN is a network segment and the router will send the data from your LAN to other locations such as your other offices, the internet, or your voice carrier. For most SMB organizations the router is provided for, and configured by your carrier. We're just mentioning to let you know it's there. You may have to pay for that, or it may be included in your charges when you sign a contract with a carrier. It's a negotiating point. It's something to keep in your mind when it comes time to talk about carrier selection which we will later on in this book.

Standardization. Your data network should become standardized to be effective. What we mean by this is that your hardware and software elements should be of the same generation, ideally of the same operating system, and your software applications need to be of current release and iden*tical from machine to machine.* We find very few businesses that have completely grasped the value of this concept, but when you standardize, your support costs go down, and perhaps more importantly, your downtime when you have issues can go down dramatically, improving productivity.

Design and Documentation

How does all this data networking get put together correctly? You need somebody to help you with the design, implement a quality installation, and very importantly, label, test, and document your data network, including the structured cable infrastructure. Software tools for discovering and inventorying your network components are widely available and not very costly. Get them, and get someone that knows how to use them. Make certain that you get a properly tested, labeled and documented cable plan as well. We meet clients all the time that never bothered to get this done at the time of installation, or if they did, haven't updated their records since. This is perfectly fine until something breaks or something changes, and something **always** breaks or changes. Their data network and voice network may have worked perfectly for five or six years, and then they decided to add 15 or 20 employees only to discover that didn't know if they had the capacity to make this change in voice and/or data hardware and software, let alone any idea about where any of the cables that connect these components came and went.

So, just because it looks great and works great on day one, know that without proper documentation and regular updates to your component inventory and infrastructure, you will pay more for repair, adds and changes in the future.

Mobile Phone Selection

Your mobile plan is going to be an extension of your overall voice and data network plan. We treat it as a separate item because the endpoint devices tend to be different, the accounting is different, often the carriers are different, and the geography tends to be different as well.

You need to have a plan for your cellphones and tablets within your business. Who gets them? Who pays for them?

Are they company owned? Are they reimbursed? Do you standardize on smartphones and basic phones?

It is also important to set a cell phone use policy. If you've chosen a system that has an app that enables smartphones to dial through the company network, are you going to enforce that? As we discussed in Chapter 2, many VoIP systems provide apps that enable the employee to dial out over the company's network, therefore displaying the company's phone number and ID, instead of the employee's private cellphone. This is an additional opportunity for branding, and it protects the relationship between the customer or prospect and the company.

Do you have a plan that certain employee categories get one kind of phone and other employees either none or a different type, and do you have any sort of mobile device management for this?

This is important. We have found that the average medium-sized company, anywhere from 15 employees to 200 or more, are in a position where their mobile phone spending has surpassed their hard-wired voice and data network spending. It's shocking, and the first time we started to become aware of this was just a few years ago. We're a bit surprised that that part of operational expenses in the average business has gotten as high as it has. This points to a significant opportunity. By getting a handle on that spending, it is possible to negotiate companywide mobile device contracts with any number of carriers.

Beyond that, there are software tools (and cloud based services) that will allow you to manage your mobile devices. Information tracked includes users, minute used, contract expiration dates, comparison of plan vs actual minutes used, etc. Some of these services will negotiate contacts with the carriers for you. Additionally, these tools will give you "find and wipe" capability—meaning simply the ability to find lost phones and tablets and to erase their contents when needed.

If you're not doing that kind of mobile device management, we can almost guarantee you that you're spending more money than you should in that part of your operational expenses for your business.

You probably will need some help in deciding whether to take on MDM, mobile device management, in-house or to use an outside service. There is a breakpoint as to whether or not an outside service will do that for you better than you might be able to do yourself. But it certainly is an area that you need to be paying close attention to.

Mobility and Wireless Technology

Mobility planning is different from your mobile phone planning. The first step is to set your policy with respect to provisioning wireless access. How much access do you want to grant your guests? What is your estimate for peak usage? Are there any company resources that you want to enable your guests to reach? How about company staff? How intensively do you estimate they will be using the wireless network?

The next step is to identify the equipment, especially WAPs and firewalls, that can support your policies. If you have articulated your needs, your IT personnel or reseller partner will be able to help with this selection. Just a few years back, wireless access in most small businesses was not much more than a little Linksys wireless router connected to a DSL circuit through your local area network to provide internet access.

Clearly, those times are gone. The components in your wireless system need to be selected correctly, and they need to be placed correctly in your facility. Your access points need to be sized and placed by an expert in this technology segment. There are tools that can be used to help you correctly predict where you need your access points placed and how many of them you might need and of what kind.

This technology is changing rapidly and our key advice to anybody upgrading or replacing or installing new wireless access systems in their building is to be certain to select the correct vendor. You need to select a manufacturer that's got some significant market share and has a plan for future product rollouts that might match your needs. Companies like Cisco Meraki and Aerohive are players that are providing products to the small business user that will allow them to correctly size, scale, administer, and secure their wireless components.

Cloud Services

Cloud Computing Applications

Selecting cloud services on the computing side will probably be an ongoing effort for your organization, and most likely will involve your IT expert as well as the staff who will be the primary users of the applications, such as data backup, virtual servers, email, accounting, CRM, and virtual desktop. The cloud services providers market is very dynamic, and you will want to have in-depth discussions with each provider.

One important aspect of selecting cloud computing services that often gets overlooked is to understand the impact that adopting the application will have on your bandwidth needs. If you are adopting an intensive application, you may need to consider increasing your bandwidth with your carrier.

Hosted VoIP

We discussed Hosted VoIP fairly extensively earlier in the book. The important consideration here is to be very clear how the hosted VoIP service is going to be delivered, and what the requirements are for your bandwidth usage. Is the hosted VoIP vendor expecting you to provide your own bandwidth, or is the vendor providing dedicated service to you? These areas are changing and you need to be aware of the changes. Selecting the best hosted VoIP vendor will require as careful consideration as any component in your communication ecosystem. Don't hesitate to ask for expert help.

Call Centers

If you've selected a cloud-based call center application, you'll need to understand the bandwidth requirements. You may have to consider the needs at your company locations, but you may also have to consider the bandwidth needs at remote workers sites if you are opting for a distributed architecture.

Video Conferencing

Video conferencing services can be as simple as Skype, GotoMeeting, or Google Hangouts on your PC or laptops, ranging up to dedicated services that allows for a higher quality experience than you might imagine is available. Video conferencing can consume an enormous amount of bandwidth, so if your organization is planning to increase its video conferencing use, be sure to evaluate both the commercial alternatives, as well estimating the impact on the bandwidth.

Video Surveillance

It's not intuitive that video surveillance might be a cloud-based service. Most people think of video surveillance is a camera outside the door hooked into a recording device in your server room accessed over your local area network by somebody's PC or laptop.

It's old school. Does it work? Yes, it does. Are there advantages to moving some of that into the cloud? Yes, there are, especially if you have a high volume requirement for video surveillance recording, and depending on your industry, you may in fact have that requirement. Archiving, and, in some respects, controlling video surveillance in the cloud is something that you're going to want to take a look at if you have that sort of requirement.

When we say video surveillance, we're really covering more than just security, you may have production environments where video recording of the processes going on in your factory are important to you. Once again, the volume and the amount of time that you need to store those video records may in fact lead you to the cloud. Again, these applications can have a significant impact on your need for bandwidth.

Bandwidth Selection

Selecting your bandwidth carrier, or carriers, can get pretty challenging these days because of the rapidly changing technical environment, as well as the availability of new services.

Voice Carrier

Let's first address your voice carrier issues. If you are upgrading your phone system to a modern VoIP system, you will likely be going with SIP trunks, as we discussed in Chapter 2, and MPLS if you have multiple locations. However, not all SIP trunks are the same, so it is imperative that you make sure that your phone system manufacturer has certified that the SIP trunk provider, the carrier, works with your manufacturer's equipment. Also, you're going to want to be certain that the new manufacturer's equipment that you're installing is going to be equipped to handle SIP and MPLS natively, and by that, we mean, without expensive gateways or without a cumbersome software reconfiguration to match up with the modern carrier offerings. Your value-added reseller can help you with this.

Even though you may be migrating to a VoIP system, you may still want to keep some of those old-school analog circuits for applications such as an alarm system or dedicated fax machine. Some of our customers even want to retain some analog circuits for emergency back-up lines. Again, discuss this topic with your prospective carrier or better yet, your value-added reseller.

Internet Carrier

By now, you should have a pretty good idea of the bandwidth you'll need for your organization, whether it's a fairly pedestrian asynchronous DSL, or a 100Gbps fiber optic connection. Here are some important related considerations.

Pricing, of course, is a very important consideration. All carriers will give you a better price for a longer term contract. It kind of makes logical sense. But do you want a longer term contract? The technology changes. In today's market, bandwidth speeds are increasing, and prices are decreasing, so it might make sense to sign a shorter term contract, such as only 1 - 2 years. In some cases, if you know fiber is coming to your neighborhood soon, you might want to just stick to a one-year contract, even though it may be more expensive.

The exception to this is whether the carrier is flexible with respect to your contract. If your prospective carrier will agree to review pricing each year during a three year contract, and if the price has come down, either lower your monthly bill, or increase your speed for the same price, then that may be the risk mitigation that you need.

Also, find out in advance what the carrier's policy is with respect to cancellations. The unfortunate reality of multiple year contracts with the carriers are that the Federal Communications Commission and the State Public Utilities Commission have allowed them to tack on very onerous termination charges, and they can be as bad as if you cancel after one year on a two-year contract, you owe them the entire second year payments that you agreed to when you signed the contract if you want to get out. So be careful.

However, some carriers have a policy that lets you cancel, and only pay the difference of what you would have paid had you originally signed a shorter term contract.

Most carriers today offer voice and data bundles. Bundling voice and data together can frequently get you a better deal, and when we say bundling voice and data together with the carrier, that can also include local and long distance minutes. It's something that you should be aware that you can negotiate. Also, if you sign anything over a one-year term on an internet circuit, you can assume that the carrier is going to provide the router for free.

Bandwidth availability is an area that's extremely complex. In the San Francisco Bay Area, there are a minimum of 50 internet bandwidth carriers offering a variety of services. The availability of the bandwidth that you would like to have depends on your physical address, and it's not something that you can go to a website and plug in your address and get a good answer for it. You're going to need help with that.

There are tools available. Your value-added reseller, if he's in the carrier business as a reseller, can help you find out with some degree of accuracy what carriers are available and how much bandwidth you can get at your particular address.

If you're moving or expanding, this is a consideration that you need to have in your plan long before you sign a lease. Not all areas of the Bay Area, a major metropolitan area, have the same sorts of availability. High speed fiber availability varies building to building in San Francisco. Ethernet over copper high speed bandwidth varies wildly by geography. You may be able to get 50 megabits of internet bandwidth in one part of Petaluma, and you might not be able to get anything more than 1.5 megabits five miles down the road. This is an area that you need to get some help with.

Whatever you decide on, you need to be sure that you've got some scalability built in. Let's say you sign a contract for an Ethernet over copper circuit that appears to have all the bandwidth you're going to need for the next three years, the term of your contract, and then you find a year into it that there's an application, a business application, that you'd like to run in the cloud that says you need twice the bandwidth. It may or may not be available at your address and the carrier that you selected may or may not be able to offer you that higher speed bandwidth. Make sure that before you sign your contract that there's a guarantee that you can scale up with the carrier without restarting your contract or without incurring onerous reinstallation charges.

We covered installation earlier, but once again, if you sign a multiple year contract, there should be a minimal amount of fees for installation. The NRCs, the nonrecurring charges, should be absorbed by the carrier in most circumstances. The router should be a part of the deal in a multiyear contract.

Another consideration is your business continuity or disaster planning. Some carriers can offer you, say, an EoC circuit, and a fixed wireless circuit. Or you may want to go with two entirely different carriers.

So how do you select the best carrier, or carriers, for your bandwidth needs? Your choices for selecting a carrier, voice and/or data, are many, probably more than you want to know about, but some of the majors include Cbeyond, TelePacific, MegaPath, XO, Comcast Time Warner, Google, AT&T, Verizon, AireSpring and many others are available to you. You can go about this selection process on your own. Every single carrier will be happy to send a sales rep to you or set up a webinar to tell you what their system is and why it might be better than the next guy. Our experience though is that this approach will end up confusing you more than helping you.

Your best approach may be to work with a value-added reseller, again like Team One Solutions, who understands what you need to support your telecom environment, and who is authorized to work with many carriers, has the tools to quickly assess the offerings available at your location, and who also knows how to best negotiate with the carriers.

Business Continuity and Disaster Recovery

The last section of technology selection for your business communications and computing ecosystem is an area we call business continuity and disaster recovery. No matter how carefully you created a plan, and selected technologies and partners, if you don't take this component into account, at some point in your business there is a risk that it will all come tumbling down. Increasingly, more businesses are being required by regulation to have specific and workable disaster recovery plans.

When considering the implications of business continuity and disaster recovery, be aware that the topic(s) touches several different technologies, both within your business and on the outside. All of your common equipment, your servers, your switches, your routers, your firewalls, your access points, and your PBXs, need to be selected in part for their ability to recover from a disaster and to maintain your business continuity, and that may be something as simple as having redundant processors, redundant hard drives within the equipment, or something a bit more sophisticated by having offsite backup for that equipment to handle your business needs in case of a disaster.

Disasters, including earthquakes, floods, hurricanes, tornadoes, and even riots, aren't the only things that can bring your telecom system down. Your business can be crippled if it's simply a backhoe cutting all the lines of communications that you've got with the outside world in the parking lot because a new building is going up next door. Your business can be interrupted by having a single server with all of your client database information on it failing and perhaps without a plan, having it be a day or a week or longer to get back up and running again. So it touches you in several different areas.

Cloud services may be able to mitigate some of the risks of loss during a disaster, but they, of course, can't totally eliminate it. The recent violent storms on our East coast effected cloud service data centers as well as individual businesses.

One of the technologies that is kind of old school, but we recommend that you have in your business, is backup power. Backup power can be in the form of UPS systems (Uninterruptible Power Supply), for your servers, your PCs, your telephone system, and in larger installations, it can even be backup generators. UPS are only good for a limited amount of time, depending on the size and number of batteries you obtain.

Let's address needs for responding to disasters with outside services. Many small and medium-sized businesses are moving away from the single carrier model to having multiple carriers. Should AT&T fail at their CO, it might be nice to have TelePacific or MegaPath or AeroSpring or some other carrier available to carry your important business data, and that works for voice as well as data.

In addition to that, you might want to consider technologies that will enable you to fail-over to remote locations, whether in your own data center or whether that's a shared space on Amazon Web Services or Rackspace, or perhaps maybe just a branch office within your own business that can take over voice and data communications should you have a disaster or a failure in the network at your one or the other locations.

This is a complex area. It's not just the technologies that you need to make sure are secure, but how they all work together. You need to take into account all of the components that will keep you up in the case of a disaster, whatever that disaster might be. The planning for this, typically speaking, is going to require a lot of thought, a lot of effort, and in some circumstances, someone from the outside world to give you a hand.

To get updates to this book and access to our videos that will show you how to grow your business with the strategies in this book, plus an invitation to interactive online livecasts to meet the author and his team, visit:

- http://os4.com/r/TEAM1, or
- text "telecom" and your email to 58885, or
- text your email address to (510) 574-7500, or
- scan this QR Code:

6 | Implementing the Plan

We've arrived at that point in the book where we can tie together everything that we've discussed and many of the things that you've accomplished in understanding why you need a telecom strategy, what your current ecosystem is, what it contains, and maybe more importantly, what it does not contain yet.

You've done your telecom inventory. You understand what you have, how much you're paying for it, how old it is, and how well it's working, and then we helped you develop a plan with your business interest in mind. What sort of plan is going to help you compete in today's marketplace?

Finally, you've selected some technologies that are going to be helpful to you in implementing your plan with the understanding that it's all tied together. There's not simply a voice plan or a data plan or a network plan, but rather a plan that includes technologies that will help you tie all of those elements together.

How are you going to go about improving your computing and communication systems in the areas where they need improvement? This chapter hopefully will give you an outline for how to accomplish that.

Timeframe

The first thing we like to advise our clients to do is to establish a timeframe. We talk with many businesses who have gotten excited about becoming more competitive with their computing and communication systems and simply never put a timeframe, a beginning and an ending, on it. That excitement tends to wear off after a while. You get buried in your day to day business and you can lose valuable time and the productivity and the savings that could come with it if you don't establish that timeframe. This doesn't mean you have to implement your entire telecom strategy at once. You may choose to stage your upgrades in over time.

Approval Process

Along with the timeframe, we suggest that you need to understand what your approval process is. Everybody in your business, small, medium or large, who is going to get involved in the benefits and the costs of making potential changes to your system needs to be identified before you put your plan together.

The stakeholders comprise every single important business unit in your company, including marketing, sales, operations, accounting, and executive management. Your plan needs to include those people, not just in the approval process, but in the understanding of what it is you're trying to accomplish.

Budget

Finally, you're going to have to arrive at an overall estimate for implementing your telecom strategy. You may choose to implement your strategy over a multi-year period. You may choose to pay cash for equipment, or you may choose to finance your equipment. Every organization's financial wherewithal, cash flow, and resources are different so you need to understand what the component costs are for your particular organization, and that's going to direct you to prioritizing the most important initiatives.

An analysis of what the costs and benefits are is extremely important: you need an ROI. We wouldn't suggest that any technology upgrade stands on its own without a positive understandable, legitimate ROI return to your business. It makes no sense to do it otherwise.

Partner Selection

Now it's time to select your vendors, selecting partners that are going to help you accomplish your plan. We'd like to think selfishly from time to time that you really need to only select one partner, and that vendor partner will end up giving you exactly what you need at the lowest possible cost, and they will be around for the life cycle of that equipment and service to make sure it's maintained and upgraded correctly.

That may be a bit hard to accomplish, but we do recommend that you focus on selecting the correct partners to work with. Up to this point, you've probably talked to several potential partners in doing an inventory of what you've got, in researching new technologies that may be appropriate. You've probably met with individual companies and partners that you've either done business with before or that you might consider doing business with in the future to implement your plan.

In addition to some of the recommendations we presented in the previous chapter, we would also advise that you probably don't want to consider companies that only have one solution to offer. Your computing and communication ecosystem is a complex multifaceted entity. You want to be certain that if you're going to make a selection among multiple manufacturers, you probably want to talk to vendors that represent more than one.

We like to work with vendors ourselves that are manufacturer agnostic. In today's computing and communication's world, there's probably no one single vendor that makes the best data switch, the best firewall, the best wireless access point, or the best PBX. Are there top leading companies? Of course, there are. You want to select partners that represent the top brands, the top manufacturers. But once again, be a little cautious of some of those providers. Sometimes their interest may not be entirely aligned with yours.

Summary

My purpose in writing this book was to shed light on what is typically a very confusing, but very important, aspect of your business: your communications ecosystem. Hopefully the book has brought some clarity to the various components of your system, provided some compelling reasons why you need to take a look at your telecommunications system, and shown you some benefits that new technologies could provide your organization.

I think it's difficult to overstate the importance of having a high functioning computing and communication systems to remain competitive in today's marketplaces, and that's probably independent of whatever type of business or organization that you have. It is just as important for traditional types of businesses to implement some of these strategies as it is for high tech companies.

My hope is that you will take action now to improve your business. Technological development will not stand still while you decide. You should take full advantage of what it has to offer—your competition certainly will.

To get updates to this book and access to our videos that will show you how to grow your business with the strategies in this book, plus an invitation to interactive online livecasts to meet the author and his team, visit:

- http://os4.com/r/TEAM1, or
- text "telecom" and your email to 58885, or
- text your email address to (510) 574-7500, or
- scan this QR Code:

Glossary

The telecom arena, like any technical field, has lots of acronyms and jargon that can easily confuse those who aren't very familiar with the language. Here are some of the terms we used throughout the book, along with a brief description.

ACD	Automatic Call Distribution. ACD is a system that distributes incoming calls to a specific group of people within an organization, based on rules that the organization has created.
Analog trunks	An analog trunk, sometimes called an analog line or business line, is a voice circuit historically made from copper wire that runs from a local phone company's Central Office (CO) to a business location.
AP	Access Point, also known as a Wireless Access Point, is a device that allows wireless devices to connect to a wired network using Wi-Fi.
Asynchronous	Asynchronous communication is the intermittent transmission of data, rather than in a steady

	stream.
Auto-attendant	Auto-attendant allows callers to be automatically transferred to an extension without the intervention of a live human being.
Business Continuity	Business continuity encompasses the plans and preparations a company makes to ensure that critical business functions will continue despite structural interruptions caused by natural disasters or man-made disruptions.
Business lines	A business line, sometimes called an analog line or analog trunk, is a voice circuit historically made from copper wire that runs from a local phone company's Central Office (CO) to a business location.
BYOB	Bring Your Own Bandwidth refers to the requirement for an organization to contract with a third-party internet services provider (ISP) in order to connect to a cloud-based service, such as hosted VoIP.
BYOD	Bring Your Own Device refers to the ability for employees or guests of an organization to be able to access network resources from their personal devices, generally using WiFi.
C7 Contractor	In the State of California, a licensed C7 Contractor is licensed to install,

	service and maintain all types of communication and low voltage systems which are energy limited and do not exceed 91 volts. These systems include, but are not limited to telephone systems, sound systems, cable television systems, closed-circuit video systems, satellite dish antennas, instrumentation and temperature controls, and low voltage landscape lighting. Low voltage fire alarm systems are specifically not included in this section.
Call center	A call center is a group inside an organization that is set up to deal with either inbound or outbound phone calls with consumers. Differs slightly from "Contact Center", which implies a wider range of media, including chat, email, etc.
Call recording	The ability to record a phone call, often required by regulation for financial and medical applications.
Carrier	A company that provides network access to residences or commercial addresses for either or both phone and data transmissions.
Cat5, Cat5e, Cat6, Cat7	These are twisted pair cables used to carry data. Current standard is Cat5e, which superseded Cat5. Cat6 and Cat7 can carry higher speeds, and provides more shielding than

	Cat5e.
CLEC	Competitive Local Exchange Carrier is a telecommunications provider who competes with the former monopoly carrier in a given geography.
Cloud	The cloud refers to offerings provided by companies who have physical servers in their data centers, and offer software, services, platforms, or infrastructure over the internet, thereby relieving their customers from the need to have physical equipment and the associated maintenance, on their site.
CO	Central Office is the physical location where a carrier has equipment that connects its customers to the public network for voice and/or data.
Coax	Also known as coaxial cable, is a specialized shielded cable that is typically used to carry cable television signals as well as internet connections.
Contact center	A contact center is a group inside an organization that is set up to deal with either inbound or outbound communication with consumers via phone, email, chat, etc. Differs slightly from "Call Center", which implies phone calls.

CPE	Customer Premise Equipment. This generally refers to centralized gear such as phone systems or data servers that are located in a customer's physical premises, as opposed to hosted in a remote location, often referred to as "in the cloud".
CRM	Customer Relationship Management refers to software applications that maintain customer records.
CTI	Computer Telephony Integration refers to applications that integrate customer databases with telephone systems, often IVR and Caller ID, so that the agent can quickly identify and act on the caller's information.
Data switch	A hardware device that interconnects devices such as computers, video cameras, and access points.
Disaster Recovery	Disaster Recovery encompasses the plans and preparations a company makes to ensure that critical business functions will recover after serious structural interruptions caused usually by natural disasters, such as storms and earthquakes, as well as human-caused disasters.
DSL	Digital Subscriber Line refers to a set of technologies that provide internet access over telephone

	wires, typically with faster download speeds than upload speeds.
EoC	Ethernet over Copper is technology that offers Ethernet speeds, often synchronous, over existing copper wires. It requires the carrier's CO to be equipped with specialized switching equipment.
ERP	Enterprise Resource Planning is business management software that enables an organization to provide a real-time view of core business processes, including manufacturing, inventory, and payroll.
Fiber	Also known as fiber optic cable is a technology that transmits data through extremely thin glass tubes. The advantage of fiber is that the signal doesn't degrade over long distance, and the speed provided is virtually unlimited. The disadvantage is that it is more expensive than copper to produce and install.
Firewall	A firewall is a network security system which provides a barrier between an organization's internal network and the internet, and analyzes data packets against a set of rules to determine what data can be allowed to pass, and which is

	to be rejected.
Fixed wireless	Fixed wireless refers to data transmission between two physical locations using microwave technology. Some carriers are setting up antennas on towers and buildings to provide an alternative means of internet access to copper and fiber.
HIPAA	Health Insurance Portability and Privacy Act is a law enacted in 1996 that provides standards for providing health insurance coverage for employees who change or lose their jobs, as well as standards for sharing medical information and the development of electronic medical records.
Hosted VoIP	Hosted VoIP is voice over IP where a service provider locates the VoIP equipment on their site, and delivers voice service to the customer over the internet.
Hybrid phone system	This is a PBX that provides different technologies for transmitting voice conversations, which can include analog, digital (or TDM), and VoIP.
Integrator	An integrator is a company that specializes in designing, engineering, and implementing a range of different technologies for end users.

ISDN	Integrated Services for Digital Network refers to a set of telecommunications standards that enable the simultaneous transmission of voice, data, video, and other network services using the PSTN.
ISP	An Internet Service Provider is an organization that provides services for accessing, using, or participating in the internet.
IVR	Interactive Voice Response is technology that enables humans to interact with a remote database application using either their voice or the tones on their telephone keypad.
LAN	A Local Area Network is a computer network that connects devices such as computers, printers, and access points in a relatively small space, typically within one physical location.
MDM	Mobile Device Management is software that secures and manages mobile devices that connect to an organization's data resources.
Measured business lines	Same as business line, sometimes called an analog line or analog trunk, is a voice circuit historically made from copper wire that runs from a local phone company's Central Office (CO) to a business

	location.
MPLS	Multi-Protocol Label Switching is a set of technologies that enable high performance data networking among nodes in a telecommunications network. It is most often used by organizations to tie numerous physical locations together.
NRC	Non-recurring charges
Patch panel	A patch panel is a piece of equipment that provides an array of jacks for ease of interconnecting, monitoring, and testing circuits.
PBX	A Private Branch Exchange is a telephone system that connects individual phones in an organization with each other and with the outside world.
PoE	Power over Ethernet is a system that passes both data and power over a single Ethernet cable of at least Cat5 or better.
POTS	Plain Old Telephone Service refers to voice grade analog transmission using copper wires to COs.
Presence	In the telecommunications world, presence refers to a set of applications that enables users on a network to detect the availability or status of other users on the network.
PRI	Primary Rate Interface is a

	telecommunications standard that divides a T1 into 23 voice channels plus one signaling channel.
PSTN	Public Switched Telephone Network refers to the infrastructure of providers and equipment that enables voice calls to be made throughout the world.
QoS	In telecommunications, Quality of Service refers to a network's ability to meet performance standards, especially with respect to response time, signal-to-noise ratios, echo, volume, and so on.
Reseller	A reseller is a company that sells products or services produced by other companies.
Router	A router is a device which directs data packets to their addressed locations in a computer network.
Server	A server is a computer that provides access to its programs or other resources over a computer network.
SIP	Session Initiation Protocol is a signaling protocol that governs telecommunications services such as voice, video, IM, presence, and fax over the IP network.
SMB	Small and Medium-sized Business
Softswitch	A softswitch is a centralized, or cloud-based, server that provides VoIP functionality.

Structured cabling	Structured cabling is the telecommunications cabling infrastructure in a physical location, consisting of the cable itself, terminations into patch panels, and cross-connects to various services, such as carriers as well as feeder cables.
Synchronous	Synchronous communications takes place in real-time, or immediately. In telecommunications, any delay in getting data packets to the recipient can seriously degrade the quality of the communications.
T1	T1 is a telecommunications signaling scheme operating at 1.54Mbps, and divided into 24 channels operating at 65kbps each.
TDM	Time Division Multiplexing is a technology that became popular in the 1980s on PBXs that were converting analog voice to digital signals.
Telco	Short for Telephone Company, or a company that provides connections to the public network through its network of COs.
Telecommunications	Also known as telecom, is the use of technology to communicate.
UC	Unified Communications is a loosely defined concept that enables communications that originate in

	one media to be received in other media. For example, having a voicemail message transcribed and sent via email, or having the audio file of the voicemail sent as an attachment to an email sent to the recipient.
UPS	Uninterruptible Power Supply is basically battery backup that provides power to systems, even after the public electrical system is unavailable.
VAR	A Value Added Reseller is usually a reseller that specializes in designing, selling, installing, and supporting products and services in which it has developed an expertise, often becoming certified by the manufacturer.
Voicemail	Voicemail enables the recording of voice messages and notifying the recipient that a voicemail has been recorded.
VoIP	Voice over Internet Protocol refers to a set of technologies that carries voice and voicemail services using Internet Protocol standards rather than the older TDM or analog signaling.
WAN	Wide Area Network refers to the linking of data networks that are usually in physically different locations.

WAP	A Wireless Access Point, also known as an Access Point, is a device that allows wireless devices to connect to a wired network using Wi-Fi.
WebRTC	Web Real Time Communications is a programming interface that enables phone calls and video chat from a web browser.
WiFi	Wi-Fi, also spelled Wifi or WiFi, is a technology that allows an electronic device to connect to the internet wirelessly.

To get updates to this book and access to our videos that will show you how to grow your business with the strategies in this book, plus an invitation to interactive online livecasts to meet the author and his team, visit:

- http://os4.com/r/TEAM1, or
- text "telecom" and your email to 58885, or
- text your email address to (510) 574-7500, or
- scan this QR Code:

Disclaimers

You further agree that our company cannot be held responsible in any way for the success or failure of your business as a result of the information presented in this book. It is your responsibility to conduct your own due diligence regarding the safe and successful operation of your business if you intend to apply any of our information in any way to your business operations.

Terms of Use

You are given a non-transferable, "personal use" license to this product. You cannot distribute it or share it with other individuals.

Also, there are no resale rights or private label rights granted when purchasing this book. In other words, it's for your own personal use only.